THE PRACTICE OF TRANQUILLITY
AND INSIGHT

THE
PRACTICE OF
TRANQUILLITY AND INSIGHT

A Guide to Tibetan Buddhist Meditation

*A commentary on the eighth chapter
of the* TREASURY OF KNOWLEDGE
by Jamgön Kongtrül

KHENCHEN THRANGU

Translated by
PETER ROBERTS

Snow Lion Publications
Ithaca, New York

Snow Lion Publications
P.O. Box 6483
Ithaca, New York 14851 USA
Tel: 607-273-8519

ISBN 1-55939-106-5

Printed in Canada on recycled paper

Library of Congress Cataloging-in-Publication Data

Thrangu, Khenchen.
The practice of tranquillity and insight: a guide to Tibetan Buddhist meditation:
a commentary on the eighth chapter of the Treasury of knowledge by Jamgön
Kongtrül / Khenchen Thrangu; translated by Peter Roberts. -- 2nd ed.
p. cm.
Includes bibliographical references and index.
ISBN 1-55939-106-5 (alk. paper)
1. Meditation--Buddhism. 2. Śamatha (Buddhism). 3. Vipaśyanā (Buddhism).
4. Buddhism--China--Tibet--Doctrines. 5. Koṅ-sprul Blo-gros-mtha'-yas 1813-1899.
Śes bya kun khyab. I. Koṅ-sprul Blo-gros-mtha'-yas 1813-1899. Śes bya kun khyab.
Selections. English. II. Title.
BQ7805.T47 1998
294.3'443--dc21 98-28051 CIP

Contents

Contents

Foreword

The foundation of Buddhist practice has always been the twofold development of gaining an understanding of the Buddha's teachings, on the one hand, and developing liberation from emotional and cognitive obscurations through the practice of meditation, on the other hand. Unfortunately, there have been few books explaining the latter process of why and how one meditates. This book by Khenchen Thrangu, Rinpoche, lays out in detail how one develops the two principal kinds of meditation—śamatha and vipaśyanā—from the stage of beginner to that of complete enlightenment.

There are, of course, many manuals on meditation, but Thrangu Rinpoche chose the *Treasury of Knowledge* for the basis of these teachings because its author, Jamgön Kongtrül, is widely known for synthesizing the knowledge and experience of many lineages in Tibet and for helping to found the Ri-me (ecumenical) movement. He is also known for writing and compiling one hundred volumes of Nyingma and Kagyü teachings. When Thrangu Rinpoche refers to "the text," he is actually referring to the eighth chapter of the first of the five books of the *Treasury of Knowledge*. This chapter has been translated by Kiki Edkelius and Chryssoula Zerbini as *The Treasury of Knowledge*. But the chapter is encyclopedic in that it encompasses the view and practice of meditation not only from the sūtra tradition but also from the mahāyāna and vajrayāna traditions. Being encyclopedic, it condenses a vast amount of information in each sentence and assumes that the reader has had extensive training in Buddhism. So, for Westerners to understand this great work, they need an extensive commentary from an accomplished scholar and Buddhist practitioner. Khenchen Thrangu is both of these.

Thrangu Rinpoche taught two seminars on this text—one at Worcester College in Oxford, England, in 1988 and the other in Kathmandu, Nepal, in 1989. To develop this text, these two seminars were recorded, transcribed, and combined into one book. The reason for combining the two different seminars was that Thrangu Rinpoche would emphasize certain points in one seminar and other points in the other seminar. Extensive editing was therefore necessary, and it is hoped that the resulting text is a thorough yet readable and understandable explanation of this very profound and complex topic.

What makes this commentary so valuable is that Thrangu Rinpoche is one of the foremost Tibetan scholars of the same Kagyü lineage to which Jamgön Kongtrül belonged. Thrangu Rinpoche was trained in Tibet, and upon leaving Tibet in 1959 he continued his studies in India. He was then examined and given the highest *geshe* degree by His Holiness the Dalai Lama. Following this he was asked by His Holiness the sixteenth Karmapa to establish the curriculum for training the Kagyü lineage and was the tutor for the four major regents: Tai Situpa Rinpoche, Gyaltsapa Rinpoche, Sharmapa Rinpoche, and Jamgön Kongtrül Rinpoche (who was a reincarnation of the author of the *Treasury of Knowledge*).

Thrangu Rinpoche is also widely recognized as being spiritually realized, and has taught thousands of students in over thirty countries. As a result, this commentary contains practical examples and insights from his experience and training rather than just an erudite explanation of the text.

Finally, to make this book more readable, Tibetan terms have been spelled according to the phonetic system. Interested readers can find the original Tibetan and transliterations in the back of the book.

CLARK JOHNSON, PH.D.

Acknowledgments

The author would like to thank the many persons who made this book possible: Peter Roberts for translating the teachings of Thrangu Rinpoche from Tibetan into English; Susan Roe and Gaby Holmann for transcribing the audio tapes of these teachings; Jean Johnson for helping to edit the manuscript; and Cornelia Hwang for organizing these teachings.

THE PRACTICE OF TRANQUILLITY
AND INSIGHT

1

INTRODUCTION TO
TRANQUILLITY AND INSIGHT
MEDITATION

THIS teaching on meditation comes from a text called the *Treasury of Knowledge,* or the *Sheja Dzo* in Tibetan. This text is called a treasury because the text has gathered together information from the *sūtras* and *tantras* and presented it in a concise form. It contains not only the actual teachings of the Buddhas, but also teachings on grammar, medicine, poetry, astrology, and other subjects. Because the text covers so much, it is also called the *Sheja Künkyab,* which means "the text that covers all knowledge."

The author of the *Treasury of Knowledge* was Jamgön Kongtrül (1813–1899). He was born to a poor family, and his father died at the time of his birth, so his family consisted of just himself and his mother. At the time there was a very powerful king of the kingdom of Derge who made his subjects do hard manual labor for him. Jamgön Kongtrül's mother told him, "There is no point in leading this kind of life, which will be mostly suffering. It is much better if you enter the *dharma* and become a monk." His mother thus sent him to a monastery, where he became ordained and studied hard and became a pupil of the ninth Tai Situpa, Pema Nyingje Wangpo. Jamgön Kongtrül was a good student and writer, and when the king of Derge heard of his skills, he wanted to make him his personal secretary. But Pema Nyingje thought, "If he is just an ordinary monk, the king will be able to take him away, and he will waste his time with temporal matters as a secretary. However, if he is declared a *tülku,* the king will not be able to have him as a secretary." The problem was that he had to be the reincarnation of someone to be identified as a tülku. So Pema Nyingje thought it would be a good idea to call him the tülku of Kongpo Pamden. This would be convenient because Kongpo Pamden had been such a good meditator. Therefore, they gave Jamgön Kongtrül the name Kongpo Pamden Tülku, and this was shortened to Kongtrül. That is how Jamgön Kongtrül got his name.

So Jamgön Kongtrül was declared a tülku and lived in a cabin on a large rock above Palpung. This rock is called Tsadra Rinchen Drak. *Rinchen drak* means "precious rock" or "jewel rock," and *tsadra* means "similar to Tsari." Tsari and Mount Kailash are two very sacred places in Tibet. Tsadra Rinchen Drak was recognized by the *tertön* Chojyur Lingpa, so this is a very special place. When one looks at the northern face of the rock, one can see the form of the deity Dorje Phurba (Skt. *Vajrakilaya*) on the rock. Jamgön Kongtrül had a little house built in the area of the heart of this form of Dorje Phurba, and he stayed there meditating in retreat. In his life story he says that he was there alone in a state of poverty, with nothing other than one bag of *tsampa* (roasted barley) and a single brick of tea.

At the time there were many lineages in Tibet—some with many lineage holders and some with only a few holders. To prevent these lineages from dying out,

Introduction

Jamgön Kongtrül collected the teachings of all these
lineages and assembled them into five texts called the
Five Treasuries. The *Treasury of Knowledge*, the work we
are dealing with here, is just one of the five. Jamgön
Kongtrül assembled these treasuries gradually. But then
it was discovered that a sūtra says, "There will come a
guide called Lodro who will teach the five kinds of
knowledge." The word *lodro* means "intelligence" in
Tibetan, and this was actually Jamgön Kongtrül's name.
The five kinds of knowledge refer to the five treasuries.
So Jamgön Kongtrül composed these five treasuries, and
great scholars have recognized the prophecy of the sūtra
as indeed being about Jamgön Kongtrül.

Jamgön Kongtrül became the teacher of the fifteenth
Karmapa, Khakhyab Dorje, which is a very special
distinction. In the *Treasury of Knowledge* are teachings on
all levels, including the sūtras and the tantras. There are
also teachings on what to do at each of these levels, how
to develop one's meditation at these levels, and so on.

Why One Should Practice Meditation

Jamgön Kongtrül begins by answering the question of
why one meditates. In Sanskrit meditation is *samādhi*, a
word translated as *ting nge dzin*[1] in Tibetan. The syllable
dzin means "to hold," and the syllable *nge* is an adverb
making the meaning "to hold something unwaveringly,
firmly, so that there is no movement." This means that
during meditation the mind does not fall under the
influence of thoughts, obscurations, or mental negativity (Skt. *kleśa*, Tib. *nyönmong*). Instead it is completely
stable and unwavering. Samādhi is translated as *gom* in
Tibetan. This word is very close to *kom*,[2] which means

3

"to become accustomed to doing something," so that it becomes a part of oneself. Meditation is very similar to familiarization because one continues meditating even if it sometimes doesn't go well. Obstacles and problems often arise, but one continues and habituates oneself to meditating until it becomes easy and natural. So through habituation one is able to remain in the state of meditation.

Samādhi includes tranquillity meditation, or *śamatha,* and insight meditation, or *vipaśyanā.* After receiving the teachings for these two types of meditation, one needs to analyze them with one's intelligence in order to gain a definite understanding of them. After gaining an understanding of these two, it is necessary to practice and meditate so that what one has learned becomes absorbed by the mind. Even if one knows a great deal about dharma, it will be of no help if one does not understand śamatha and vipaśyanā meditation. Therefore, one must practice meditation so that what is conceptually learned becomes a part of oneself. Thus we must examine meditation first.

There are several levels of understanding. From hearing the Buddhist teachings one develops the *understanding of listening*; from thinking about these teachings one develops the *understanding of contemplation.* These two are not enough to develop full understanding because one must turn one's mind inward to gain the understanding that comes from meditation. Instead of focusing the mind externally by listening to the teachings, one focuses one's attention internally on the mind itself to develop *understanding of meditation.* One cannot benefit much from focusing on external phenomena because the mind is bound up by the kleśas, and the only way

Introduction

to free oneself from the bondage of kleśas is to turn inward through meditation. Jamgön Kongtrül gives two examples illustrating the necessity for meditation. One is the example of a farmer. For a farmer to be happy and well fed, he must plant a field, work hard, and get a good harvest. To have a good crop in the field is not enough; he must harvest it and eat it. Similarly, just listening to the teachings and contemplating them is not enough; one must meditate to dispel the negativity in one's mind and develop inner wisdom. In the second example, borrowed from Śāntideva, a doctor must have knowledge of the medicines and their proper application, which is gained through the study of medical books. But just reading medical books will not eliminate disease; the patient must take the medicines described in the texts. Similarly, just listening to and contemplating the dharma is not enough because it will not quell the kleśas and calm the mind. To develop the qualities of wisdom, one must practice meditation. To practice meditation means to habituate oneself to meditation. If one's mind is peaceful and happy in ordinary life, all external things appear pleasant and attractive; if one's mind is disturbed and unhappy, all these external things seem unpleasant and not right. One needs to make the mind peaceful and happy to develop inner wisdom, and this is done by meditation.

Samādhi, the state of deep meditation, is composed of two elements: śamatha and vipaśyanā. There are, in fact, a great number of meditation techniques, but they can all be included in these two categories. In the *Definite Explanation of the View* sūtra the Buddha says there are the samādhis of the *śrāvakas,* who are the

5

followers of the *hīnayāna*, and there are the samādhis of the *bodhisattvas*, who are the followers of the *mahāyāna*, and there are the samādhis of the *tathāgatas* (the buddhas), who have followed meditation to its completion. All these can be included in two kinds of samādhis: śamatha and vipaśyanā. Having understood that all meditation comes from śamatha and vipaśyanā, one should prepare oneself to do these meditations. One should also seek out specific instructions to practice them. The purpose of practicing śamatha and vipaśyanā in the hīnayāna is to achieve happiness and various special qualities. In the mahāyāna the purpose of meditation is to benefit all beings, so this view has a wider viewpoint and requires greater motivation. This is why the mahāyāna is called the "greater" vehicle. In Buddhism the results of the hīnayāna and the mahāyāna come from the practice of śamatha and vipaśyanā. The attaining of day-to-day happiness is also the result of śamatha and vipaśyanā.

Many individuals whom I have met in my extensive travels in Europe and North America have told me their private problems—mental problems, physical problems, and unhappiness with their possessions or their work. The answer to the multitude of these problems is always the same: to make one's mind peaceful and calm and develop understanding and wisdom. So ordinary worldly happiness comes down to practicing śamatha and vipaśyanā. The *Definite Explanation of the View* sūtra says that the root of the accomplishment of the goal of all worldly and spiritual activity is śamatha and vipaśyanā meditation. This sūtra consists of the Buddha and Maitreya conversing in the form of questions and answers. In this sūtra the Buddha says to Maitreya that whatever worldly or spiritual qualities are possessed by the śrāvakas, the bodhisattvas, or the tathāgatas are all the result of śamatha and vipaśyanā. This explains the importance of śamatha and vipaśyanā because they are the root of all meditation. Knowing this, one should develop a great interest in practicing these two kinds of meditation.

The Essential Nature of Śamatha and Vipaśyanā

Śamatha is actually the mind resting one-pointedly on an object so that not many thoughts arise and the mind becomes very stable and calm. The mind rests in peace. The Tibetan for *śamatha* is *shi-ne,* meaning "peace."[3] So śamatha is "resting in peace." Simply keeping the mind one-pointed is not śamatha meditation because in true śamatha, the object one focuses on should be something positive. A negative object would be something that causes attachment, aggression, or ignorance to arise in the mind, making it unable to rest calmly on something. Resting on something genuinely positive allows the mind to rest in peace. Śamatha is practiced to prevent the arising of so many thoughts. One might think that śamatha is a state of no thoughts, perhaps like that of a stone. This is incorrect because in śamatha meditation the mind is very calm and stable and also very clear so that it can distinguish and discriminate between all phenomena and see everything as very distinct. This clarity is called vipaśyanā, or *insight,* and is developed through śamatha.

The nature or identity of śamatha is described in the *Cloud of Jewels* sūtra. It says that if one's mind has many thoughts, one cannot focus on the object of attention.

7

The mind cannot focus on something because of the distraction of thoughts. If the mind can focus one-pointedly without this distraction, one has śamatha meditation. The sūtra also says that vipaśyanā has the clarity of understanding in which everything is seen clearly and distinctly; the relative is seen as relative, the absolute as absolute. So the actual nature of things is seen as it is, and this is what is meant by vipaśyanā. A commentary on the *Cloud of Jewels* sūtra was composed by Vasubandhu, who was a great master of the *abhidharma*. Vasubandhu said that in genuine śamatha the mind is able to rest in the mind. The mind becomes so relaxed that it rests in itself, just as it is, in a natural way, undistracted by thoughts. "Distracted" in Tibetan is *yengwa,* which means "swept away." The word *distracted* in this context has in it the connotation of being carried away with no control by a strong river. In the same way, one's mind cannot stay still and is just carried away. If the mind is resting in the mind, it is just where it is, and the mind becomes stable and peaceful and relaxed. The *Cloud of Jewels* sūtra says, "Śamatha is the one-pointed mind," and Vasubandhu's commentary explains that vipaśyanā is "the discrimination of phenomena," meaning that all things appear as very clear and distinct from one another. So this is the nature of vipaśyanā. With śamatha and vipaśyanā one has a genuine state of meditation with the mind resting in mind and being able to distinguish all phenomena. Without śamatha and vipaśyanā one does not have a genuine samādhi or meditation state.

The third text cited by Jamgön Kongtrül comes from Kamalaśīla. In the eighth century Śāntarakṣita came to Tibet and taught the stages of meditation. Owing to his clairvoyance, he knew that he would soon pass away. So he said, "I have given these teachings. In the future, problems may occur and things might go wrong. When this happens, invite my pupil Kamalaśīla from India. He will be able to explain meditation clearly and remove any errors in interpretation that might arise." This was his last wish, and then he passed away.

Then from China a Chinese master named Hashang Mahāyāna came to Tibet and said, "You have been receiving these teachings from Śāntarakṣita, but these teachings are on the gradual path. This is not the profound way and is very difficult to do and takes a long time. My teachings are the instantaneous way and are easier and faster than the gradual way. Whether a good thought or a bad thought comes to mind makes no difference. If one has a white cloud, it obscures the sun; if one has a black cloud, it also obscures the sun. If one is bitten by a white dog, one will have teeth marks; if one is bitten by a black dog, one will also have teeth marks. If a good thought arises, it is not good; if a bad thought arises, it is not bad. Instead one needs to rest in a state of no thoughts whatsoever." Such are the teachings he gave, and the people of Tibet became confused and did not know the correct way to meditate. Then they remembered what Śāntarakṣita had said and invited Kamalaśīla from India to clear up these misunderstandings.

In fact, there is nothing wrong with Hashang's teachings except that they did not include the development of love and compassion and the accumulation of merit through good actions. In his system, one just stopped all thoughts and meditated. When Kamalaśīla arrived in Tibet, he wanted to know whether Hashang was intelligent or not. If he wasn't intelligent, then there wouldn't be any point in debating with him. Now, near Samye Monastery in Tibet is the great Tsangpo River, which is actually the upper part of the Brahmaputra River. It is very wide. On one side of the river stood Kamalaśīla and on the other side, Hashang Mahāyāna. To determine how intelligent Hashang was, Kamalaśīla took his staff and whirled it above his head three times. This was to symbolically ask the question, "Where do the three realms of *saṃsāra* come from?" Hashang Mahāyāna was intelligent and held up his two hands, which were covered by the long sleeves of his cloak. This meant, "They come from ignorance, which grasps the dualism of perceiver and perception." When Kamalaśīla saw this answer, he set up a debate to be held at Samye Monastery. The king of Tibet presided over the debate and brought flower garlands. The king said that previously the *mahāpaṇḍita* Śāntarakṣita had come and given teachings; later Hashang Mahāyāna came and gave teachings that were not the same as Śāntarakṣita's. The king then said, "I am just an ordinary being and cannot tell who is correct, so we will have a debate in which you will ask each other questions. If someone is defeated in the debate, he should give these garlands to the victor. He should then accept defeat gracefully and leave quietly without any fuss or resentment." They then held a debate asking each other questions. In the end Hashang Mahāyāna lost the debate and presented the flower garlands to Kamalaśīla. When this was done, Kamalaśīla gave teachings on meditation that can be found in his *Stages of Meditation*. In the *Treasury of Knowledge* the explanation of śamatha and vipaśyanā follows the teaching of Kamalaśīla.[4]

Introduction

The second volume of the *Stages of Meditation* describes the nature of śamatha meditation. In śamatha the mind is continuously focused inward so that it becomes very peaceful and all external distractions are pacified. The obstacle to śamatha is external distractions such as sight, sound, and taste. The development of śamatha occurs when the mind is continuously turned inward and naturally rests in that state. Kamalaśīla says that there are two characteristics that arise from śamatha. The first characteristic is attraction to śamatha because one feels it is important and naturally does it because of a state of joy. The second is that the mind is "completely trained," which means one isn't battling with thoughts or distractions. One can rest one's mind on what one wishes without any conflict. So these are the two qualities of śamatha meditation.

In summary, when one achieves śamatha, one is not in a state of dullness or stupor. When śamatha is developed, one eliminates distracting thoughts that keep one from being able to examine or analyze things. Removing the distraction of thoughts leads to perceiving things very clearly and distinctly, which is vipaśyanā. This is how Kamalaśīla describes the nature of śamatha and vipaśyanā.

Etymology of Śamatha and Vipaśyanā

The Sanskrit word for *śamatha* was translated into Tibetan as *shi-ne*. This was a literal translation because the first two syllables, *śama,* mean "peace," and the Tibetan *shiwa* also means "peace." This peace means that the mind is not distracted because when the mind is overcome with anger, sadness, regret, or craving, it becomes distracted. But in śamatha the mind is very relaxed and at ease without any difficulties or hardships. The third syllable, *tha,* means "to dwell" or "stability." In Tibetan "to dwell" is *nepa.* In this context it means that the mind is not involved in forced activity or difficulties but dwells in a state of peace. In Tibetan this is the *ne* in *shine.* There are many different kinds of samādhis, or meditative states, but śamatha is the basis of all the meditative states in which the mind is resting onepointedly on something and remains completely focused on that object.

The Sanskrit word *vipaśyanā* is made up of two parts. The first part, *vi,* is short for *viśeṣa,* which means "special," "superior," or "particular." The second part, *paśyanā,* means "to see" or "to look." So *vipaśyanā* means "to look at things in a very direct way, in an especially clear way." It is seeing with the eyes of wisdom. This was translated into Tibetan as *hlagtong,* where *hlag* means "special" and *tong* means "to see."

The Necessity of Both Śamatha and Vipaśyanā

One might think that it is possible to practice śamatha alone or practice vipaśyanā without doing any śamatha. But in fact, whatever Buddhist practices one does, one must practice both śamatha and vipaśyanā meditation together. This is illustrated by the example of a butter lamp, which Tibetans used in the past to illuminate the darkness. A butter lamp's light is very clear and bright. For a lamp to give light it must have the qualities of being steady and not blown by the wind. If the flame is not bright or steady, one won't see things in the dark. In the same way, to see the true nature of phenomena, one has to have a clear understanding and be able to focus the mind on the object for as long as is necessary. If either of these is missing, then the true nature of things cannot be perceived. One needs to have both śamatha (the unwavering light) and vipaśyanā (the bright flame). With both, one has complete freedom to focus on anything and is able to eliminate all kleśas and develop the wisdom that one needs. If one practices śamatha meditation without vipaśyanā, one will not be able to understand the true nature of phenomena; one will just be able to rest the mind on something. It is like being on a vacation; one experiences peace on a vacation, but one does not get any lasting results from it.

If you practice vipaśyanā without śamatha, you will not be able to eliminate whatever negativity needs to be eliminated, because vipaśyanā without śamatha is unstable. So even if you have the understanding of vipaśyanā, your mind will be agitated. Therefore, you need to have both śamatha and vipaśyanā. This has been said by the Buddha in the sūtras and also in the *vajrayāna* teachings.

The Progressive Order of Meditation

The next question is: Does one start with śamatha, or with vipaśyanā, or with both at the same time? The answer is that one starts with śamatha and then does vipaśyanā practice because śamatha is the basis of meditation and vipaśyanā is based upon śamatha. In the example of the butter lamp, śamatha is like the butter or oil and vipaśyanā is like the wick placed in the oil. If one doesn't have any oil and tries to light the lamp, one won't get a good flame. But if one has oil in the lamp, one gets a good steady, bright flame. Similarly, one needs to establish śamatha meditation and then develop vipaśyanā meditation.

Śāntideva was a great scholar and *siddha* in India who, being blessed by Mañjuśri, composed *A Guide to the Bodhisattva's Way of Life*. In this work he describes each of the six perfections, or *pāramitās*. Śāntideva says one needs to have vipaśyanā that is based on śamatha meditation—a very peaceful śamatha—to which one has become completely familiarized and accustomed. If we have vipaśyanā that possesses this very good śamatha meditation, we will be able to overcome the kleśas. Therefore, we need to begin first with śamatha meditation. In the chapter on the pāramitā of meditation, Śāntideva says the essence of vipaśyanā is seeing all things undistractedly and very clearly. This discriminating wisdom (Skt. *pratyaveksanāprajñā*) sees relative phenomena as being relative.

So with discriminating wisdom we can see the actual, true nature of mind, just as it is. But before this can happen, our mind must be workable, which means that we can do whatever we want with the mind—if we want to send it somewhere, it will go; if we want to leave it in a particular spot, it will stay there. As we know from experience, our mind normally acts as if it belongs to someone else—it just wanders off somewhere by itself. So we need to have complete control of our mind in order to see the nature of things with the understanding of vipaśyanā.

PART ONE

TRANQUILLITY
[*zhi gnas*]

2

ŚAMATHA: TRANQUILLITY MEDITATION

The Prerequisites for Practicing Śamatha

There are favorable conditions for meditation, and if these are present, śamatha will develop. If they are absent, no śamatha will develop.

When the dharma was first introduced into Tibet in the seventh century, there was a good understanding and practice of the dharma. Later Langdarma, a king of Tibet, suppressed the dharma in the tenth century and destroyed much of the Buddhist teachings. After this destruction, some of the dharma was preserved, but some of the preserved teachings were incorrectly practiced. As a result the Tibetans were no longer sure who was giving the correct teachings. So in 1042 Atīśa was invited to Tibet from India because he was believed to be the most qualified person to teach the correct way of practicing. Atīśa also received a revelation and prophecy from Tārā saying that if he went to Tibet, this would be of great benefit to the dharma.

Upon arriving in Tibet, Atīśa gave teachings on the methods of śamatha and vipaśyanā meditation. These teachings can be found in his book *Lamp for the Path to Enlightenment*. In this text he says that to do śamatha meditation one needs to have favorable conditions. Even if one is diligent and applies oneself for many years to śamatha meditation, if these favorable conditions are lacking, one will fail to develop real śamatha meditation. However, he also says that if all the favorable conditions are present and one concentrates the mind on something good and positive, then one will be able to accomplish śamatha meditation and be able to develop clairvoyant powers.

In his second volume of the *Stages of Meditation* Kamalaśīla says that (1) one should reside in a favorable place—a place where one can obtain the materials one needs. In terms of mind, (2) one shouldn't have a great deal of desire, thinking, "Oh, I need this to meditate; no, I need two or three things to meditate," and so on. This kind of thinking will only create an obstacle. (3) One must also be content, which means whatever one has is fine and all right. (4) One should also give up activities such as business or buying and selling so that (5) one can have pure, good conduct. So, (6) when one stays and meditates in this place, it is completely correct. (7) One should also avoid any distractions or desires that appear as well as ideas and concepts. This, then, is a list of seven conditions necessary for the development of śamatha.

In the *Ornament of the Mahāyāna Sūtras,* Maitreya says that we should practice where we can easily obtain the necessities such as clothing, food, and so on. The place where we stay should be free from thieves or any fear of danger. We should be in a healthy place that is not extremely cold or hot or damp and will not impair our health. We also need good companions who have the same view and behavior as ourselves. If they have a different view or way of life, they will prevent us from gaining stability of mind. The place where we stay should also be free from a lot of activity and a large number of people. These are the outer conditions of where we should stay. This sūtra also describes the inner conditions of mind, namely, lack of desire, contentment, and reducing involvement in too many activities. Finally, it describes the point between mind and the outer world, which is our conduct or behavior. We should have peaceful and gentle conduct in accordance with the *prātimokṣa* vows or the bodhisattva vow. The prātimokṣa vows are prohibitions against such acts as killing, stealing, and adultery. The main idea is that if we do any of these negative actions, our mind will not be able to rest in a natural peaceful state. In terms of the bodhisattva vow, if we have anger, jealousy, aversion, and so on, then our mind will not be able to rest in a peaceful state. Instead, we need to develop love and compassion for all sentient beings. So if this interface between inner and outer leads to benefiting other beings, then favorable conditions for śamatha will develop.

Categories of Śamatha

There are four kinds of śamatha meditation. The first is called *desire realm* śamatha. One makes the mind so relaxed that it becomes completely stable and peaceful. Next is *dhyāna* śamatha, or śamatha of mental stability of the *form realm*. One has an intense experience of joy or bliss with this kind of meditation. The third kind is *formless realm* śamatha, in which everything disappears. The fourth kind is the *cessation* śamatha, which isn't practiced very much today, but in previous times some śrāvakas of the hīnayāna used to do this practice and reach a state where mind ceases and mental continuity stops.

More precisely, there are nine stages of śamatha. First, in the desire realm, there is the *one-pointed* śamatha, which means that one does not have complete mental stability, but one has a certain amount of mental stability so that one is not distracted by external objects. Next, in the form realm, there are four successive levels of śamatha meditation. The first is śamatha with *examination and analysis*. The second is śamatha with *joy and bliss*. The third is śamatha with *inhalation and exhalation*. And the fourth level is śamatha that is *free from the eight defects*. The first two defects are (1) the physical suffering of the desire realm and (2) the mental suffering of the desire realm. The remaining six are defects of the previous three levels of śamatha in the form realm: (3) analysis, (4) examination, (5) joy, (6) bliss, (7) inhalation, and (8) exhalation. Freedom from inhalation and exhalation means that in that state one is completely still without any breathing. So there are these four levels of śamatha meditation in the form realm.

There are four states of meditation that belong to the formless realm, which is a state like that of emptiness, but not the emptiness (*śūnyatā*) of the Madhyamaka. It is just a void or blank in which nothing is perceived or focused on. There are four stages of śamatha in this formless realm. These are the śamatha of *infinite space,* the śamatha of *infinite consciousness,* the śamatha of *neither existence nor nonexistence,* and the śamatha of *nothing whatsoever.* All together, then, there are nine stages of śamatha meditation: one in the desire realm, four in the form realm, and four in the formless realm.

Śamatha: Tranquillity Meditation

Posture

There are two ways to describe posture during meditation: the seven aspects of posture of Vairocana and the five aspects of dhyāna meditation. In this section I shall describe the seven aspects of Vairocana. *Vairocana* means "what illuminates, what makes clear." So Vairocana is the physical posture of sitting that helps one develop a meditative state and makes the mind stable and clear. Whether the mind becomes unstable depends on what are called the airs or subtle winds (Skt. *vayū*, Tib. *lung*). There is the gross air, which is the breath one inhales and exhales. But there is also a subtle air, which is involved with the movements of the body and the movement of thoughts. Body and mind are related, so when these subtle airs become still in the body, the mind also becomes still. One makes these subtle airs stable by working on the inner channels (Skt. *nāḍī*, Tib. *tsa*) through which the airs move. If these channels are straight and stable, the subtle airs will become stable, and then the mind will become stable. To make these channels straight and stable, one must have proper posture during meditation.

There are several different kinds of subtle airs, or *vayūs*. The subtle air that makes the body stable and firm is the *subtle air of earth*. The subtle air that keeps the body warm is the *subtle air of fire*. The subtle air that keeps the body from drying up is the *subtle air of water*. The subtle air that spreads warmth throughout the whole body and causes physical movement is called the *subtle air of air* (the *lung* of *lung* in Tibetan). So one has a subtle air for each of the four elements. There is also a fifth, *downward-eliminating air,* which transforms the food in the stomach, separates the waste matter from the food, and expels the waste through the anus.[5]

The first aspect of the Vairocana posture is (1) keeping the spine straight so that the central energy channel is straight. The life-force vayū is called *prāṇa* (Tib. *soklung*) and flows in the central channel. Prāṇa makes one's body stable and firm. It is also called the earth vayū because it gives stability and endurance to the body. If the body is bent forward in meditation, or leaning to the left, right, or backward, then this central channel is going to be bent and the prāṇa flowing within it will be constricted. Therefore if one keeps the spine straight, the earth vayū will flow straight, and this will result in endurance and stability.

The water vayū permeates the body and keeps it moist. If these water vayūs flow in the central channel, they will naturally be stable. In order to cause the water vayū to flow in the central channel, (2) one places the hands in a meditative posture (3) with the elbows slightly sticking out. The fire vayū naturally goes upward, while the earth and water vayū naturally go downward. For the fire vayū to enter the central channel, (4) one lowers the chin slightly, which has the effect of preventing the fire vayū from rising upward.

To introduce the air vayū into the central channel, (5) one's eyes should be unwavering. The air vayū is connected with movement of the body, and the eyes naturally have a great deal of movement associated with them. The moving of the eyes will cause the mind to move. So one keeps the eyes still, focused on the space beyond the tip of the nose. This will cause the mind to become still and the air vayū to enter the central channel. (6) The lips are also left to rest quite naturally, with the tongue resting against the palate. To stabilize the down-ward-eliminating vayū, (7) one sits with one's legs in the *vajra* (full-lotus) posture.

The first five aspects of posture relate to the five vayūs, but the air vayū has two aspects, the eyes and the lips. The water vayū also has two aspects, with the hands in the meditation posture and the upper arms being extended, totaling seven aspects of meditation posture. Many instructions say that one should expel the dead air three times before beginning meditation because with normal breathing, one's body accumulates impure or negative air. To get rid of this, one exhales with more force than usual, but not with a great deal of force. While doing this, one thinks that all the mental negativities, the kleśas, are being exhaled with the breath, and one inhales in a very relaxed way. This is done three times: first with slightly greater strength than normal, second with still greater strength, and third with even more strength. After this one breathes normally, very relaxed, thinking that one has expelled all the negativities.

The hands in meditation should be resting in the meditation posture or literally "resting in the equality posture." You can rest the right hand on top of the left hand because "resting equally" means your hands are at the same level, so that if one hand is on the knee, then the other should be on the other knee at the same level. It doesn't make any difference; use whichever one you find comfortable.

In the *mahāmudrā* tradition of the vajrayāna, the seven aspects of the posture of Vairocana just discussed are usually given. But Jamgön Kongtrül uses the eight aspects of posture given by Kamalaśīla in his *Stages of*

23

Meditation. To begin with, you should sit comfortably and follow these eight points.

First, your legs should be fully crossed in the vajra posture or in the semi-crossed (half-lotus) posture. You should be relaxed; you don't have to force yourself into the vajra posture. In the West not everyone can sit cross-legged. Some people sit with the knees sticking up, but eventually the knees will come down. This is accomplished with the achievement of suppleness of body. It is better to sit comfortably than to sit in pain.

Second, your eyes should be half-closed, which means they should be neither wide open and staring ahead nor fully closed so that everything is dark. They are kept half-closed without any effort or tension so that they are completely relaxed and you don't have to think about them.

Third, the upper body should be straight. Since the body and mind are interconnected, if the body is straight, these channels are straight, the subtle energies will flow smoothly in them, and the mind will become still and stable. If the body is bent, the channels become blocked and the mind is adversely affected because some channels will have little energy moving in them and other channels will have rapidly moving energy, which results in a host of thoughts arising in the mind.

Fourth, the shoulders should be level and the body upright, and you should not lean to the left or right.

Fifth, you should be looking downward toward the nose. Your gaze should be toward the nose so that you are aware of your nose. The classical description is that the gaze should be four finger-widths beyond the nose.

Sixth, there should be a slight gap between the lips

and teeth because if the teeth are held against one another, they can create grinding sounds.

Seventh, the tongue should be against the palate. Otherwise, saliva will accumulate in the mouth and you will be distracted by swallowing.

Finally, the breathing should be effortless and natural. You should not try to suppress the breath or force deep breaths.

Each of these eight aspects of posture, such as keeping the eyes half-closed, may individually seem rather unimportant, but to develop complete clarity and stability of mind, all these aspects of posture are actually important because each has a special purpose in bringing about stability and clarity.[6]

Four Objects of Meditation

There are two explanations of how to hold the mind in meditation. The first is a general description, and the second is a specific set of stages of meditation.

In the general explanation, the Buddha taught that there are four classes of objects of meditation. The first is the *all-pervasive object* of meditation. It is so called because it applies to all phenomena. This object can be focused on without analysis, with the mind simply resting, or with analysis, where one is looking at either the actual nature of phenomena or their relative multiplicity.

The second class of objects of meditation is the *pacification of behavior*. This is meditation that purifies faults. Where do these negative patterns come from? In the Buddhist teaching, our present life originates from a previous life. That previous life came from a life before that, and so on. During our present life, we can experience physical pain and mental suffering, or we can experience happiness and bliss. These experiences come from our actions in a previous life. They are the result of *karma*. However, not everything is due to karma. Some people have great desire or great anger, and this might come from the power of habituation in a previous life and not as a result of karma. One might have become habituated to desire or anger, and these emotions become greater and greater, so that in the next life there will be great desire or great anger. Or in one lifetime we may encounter a remedy for this desire or anger, and this will lessen our faults, which may continue to lessen through successive lifetimes. So if we were accustomed to a lot of desire in our previous lives, then there will be a lot of desire in our present life. If we were accustomed to a lot of anger in our previous lives, we will experience a lot of anger in this lifetime. If we were accustomed to having many thoughts in our previous lives, our present mind will not be able to remain stable; thoughts will take over our mind, and we will be under their power. Finally, if we had strong ignorance in our previous lifetime, we will have become accustomed to this, and our present mind will contain a lot of ignorance. So these patterns describe the five types of persons (those with great attachment, anger, ignorance, jealousy, and pride), and meditation is done to remedy these five kinds of mentality.

If we have strong desire and attachment to our own body or to external things, we can practice meditation on ugliness. We normally see our body as solid, lasting, and important; but the Buddha taught that we have a precious human existence, which allows us to practice the dharma and benefit other beings. It is a precious human existence, but the body itself is not precious. We meditate on the object of our attachment, seeing that it is not beautiful, solid, or lasting. This lessens our attachment.

If we have a great deal of anger, we meditate on love or compassion, which will lessen our anger. Anger normally is the desire to harm someone else. Instead we do the meditation of taking our own body as an example for all other beings. Normally, if we experience the slightest amount of pain, it is undesirable, and if we experience the slightest pleasure or comfort, it is desired. So, in this meditation we should think that all other beings are like our own body: disliking suffering and desiring the experience of pleasure and happiness. There isn't anyone who likes to experience suffering. So thinking of the sameness of other beings to our own body, we will develop love for beings, and lose the wish to cause harm or pain to others, which will lessen our anger.

There are two kinds of ignorance: distinct and indistinct ignorance. Indistinct ignorance is always there and present with other mental events. It accompanies the arising of all the negativity of mind such as anger, pride, attachment, and so on. Being ignorant, one is not aware of what is good and what is harmful. As these different mind poisons arise, their nature is not understood, and one doesn't know if they are good or bad. As a result they are ever-present, but they are not distinct from ignorance itself. The second kind of ignorance, distinct ignorance, is an isolated ignorance, an ignorance resulting from not having received or contemplated the Buddhist teachings. Through learning and contemplation, gradually this ignorance can be removed. If one has a great deal of ignorance, the remedy in terms of śamatha meditation is contemplation on the twelve links of dependent origination. One contemplates how all things arise and depend on something else. For example, by being accustomed to doing good actions and having good thoughts, the power of habit will cause good thoughts and actions to occur. Similarly, when the mind is accustomed to negativity and bad things, through the power of that habit negative thoughts and actions occur. So all things are interdependent and contemplation on dependent origination is the remedy for ignorance.

The remedy for pride is to meditate on the elements that make up a being. With pride one thinks of oneself as superior or special. The remedy is to meditate on the five aggregates (Skt. *skandhas*). By thinking of oneself as special or superior, one sees oneself as solid and definite. If one examines the aggregates, one discovers that things are not solid, but always changing. One is just an aggregation of different elements. For example, a person is made up of the five aggregates collected together or just an aggregation of different parts. So, being aware of the five aggregates will diminish one's pride.

The remedy for having too many thoughts is to meditate on one's breath. By meditating on the breath, which is quite subtle and changing all the time with the in-and-out movements, one's thoughts become less and less strong. So this is the remedy for too many thoughts.

The third class of objects of meditation is the *objects of the learned* and is the understanding of the five aggregates. For example, one learns that the body is a mass of parts; it is made up of the five aggregates of form, sensation, identification, mental activity, and consciousness. One learns that the mind is not just a single indivisible unit, but a composite. There are the eighteen elements that have to do with its organization. For example, the eye originates from the eye of a previous moment. Then there is the understanding of the twelve āyatanas that are involved in organization and development. For example, one learns how the eye and visual consciousness connect with some external object and how visual perception occurs through this connection. So the sense organ, the object, and the consciousness must come together for perception to occur. One then learns how the twelve steps of dependence origination work. Finally, one learns the study of the appropriate and the inappropriate, which is a list of things that could and could not happen due to certain causes. So the contemplation of these things is called the contemplation of the learned.

The fourth class of objects of meditation is the *purification of the kleśas*. One contemplates the peaceful state in which śamatha is present and the opposite state in which śamatha is absent. Through vipaśyanā there is the understanding of the causes of saṃsāra and the causes of nirvāṇa. All together there are sixteen aspects related to the four noble truths.

Four Obstacles to Meditation

There are four kinds of thoughts that cause obstacles to one's meditation. These are malicious thoughts, which are the wish to harm someone, thoughts of jealousy, thoughts of doubt and uncertainty, and thoughts of attachment and craving. For example, if thoughts of aggression come up, one needs to recognize them because they will return continuously in one's meditation. One must recognize that aggression, when one becomes attached to it, is causing harm to one's meditation. The main thing is that one should not be involved in or attached to the thoughts. If one is not attached to the thoughts, it will be easy to get rid of them. But if one is attached to these thoughts, it will be very difficult to get rid of them.

There are two different kinds of thoughts: gross and subtle. When gross thoughts arise in meditation, one forgets that one is meditating and loses one's mindfulness and awareness. Then one remembers, "Oh, I am meditating" and returns to meditating. These gross thoughts are called an actual distraction. The way to prevent these gross thoughts is to retain mindfulness and awareness. The second kind are subtle thoughts, called thoughts that come from below. With these one does not forget that one is meditating, but remains there thinking, "These little thoughts are occurring." These thoughts are so small that one cannot usually do very much about them and they are very difficult to get rid of. These thoughts don't particularly harm meditation; they just come up in one's awareness and one just leaves them as they are and eventually one will be able to eliminate them. These little thoughts, however, can sometimes gradually grow larger and larger, and one's meditation is lost. So, first one is aware of these little thoughts, then one gets distracted by them and one's mindfulness is lost. One should try to prevent this from happening by having a very stable and enduring mindfulness and awareness because this awareness is necessary with each successive instant. If one can do that, one will not be distracted.

The Specific Stages of Meditation

There are three basic kinds of śamatha meditation in relation to the object of meditation. First is *meditation with an external object,* second is *meditation without an external object,* and third is *meditation on the essential nature of things.*

You begin śamatha meditation by trying to make your mind stable and clear. But you are not accustomed to meditation, so you lose the meditation. Therefore in the beginning you need an object to meditate on. In the same way that a child needs to learn the alphabet before reading a book, so in the beginning you meditate with an object and gradually move on to meditate without an object. The first meditation is on an object: place in front of you a piece of wood or stone that is small and focus your mind on it. In doing this meditation, you should have the proper tension, that is, the proper amount of focusing. It should not be too tense or too loose. As Saraha says, meditation should be like a Brahmin's thread. In the past it was the Brahmin caste's job to make thread. To make the thread properly, one had to have the proper tension. If the tension was too tight, the thread would knot up; if it was too loose, it would easily break. To develop mental stability you begin with your attention on an object—first an impure object, and later you introduce a pure object such as a statue of the Buddha or a deity's insignia or a special syllable. The purpose of meditation on a pure object is not to develop devotion or compassion; you just rest

31

your mind on it to develop concentration. You should also not think about the faults or the good qualities of the object you are focusing on. You begin with a stone or piece of wood because it does not have any features. A Buddha image, however, has many different features—eyes, ears, and so on—to distract you.

The second type of śamatha meditation is *meditation without an external object*. The mind turns inward and focuses on a mental image of the Buddha in the form of a yidam deity such as Avalokiteśvara (Tib. Chenrezi). You either place the image mentally above your head, visualize it in front of you, or visualize that your own body is the deity. Because you are unable to imagine the entire form at first, you first imagine the deity's hand, then the eyes, then the clothes, and so on. Imagining just the parts is called "partial meditation without an object." By doing this again and again you eventually become familiar with the visualization and eventually you are able to imagine the entire form of the deity. Next you see all parts of the deity in a general way so you have a general picture of the entire body. This is called "having visualization of the complete object." Some individuals expect to get a very clear image of the deity in their meditation, and when this does not occur, they become disappointed. The eye or visual faculty has the visual consciousness that "sees" things extremely clearly. However, in meditation you use the mental consciousness, which has a general impression of things or a general idea or meaning of things so you don't get as clear a perception as with visual consciousness. So you shouldn't have the expectation of visualizing the deity as clearly as if you were actually looking at a picture of the deity. You should not be concerned with the clearness of the image because the purpose of meditation is not to get a clear image, but to focus the mind on the image so the mind will become still and stable.

The master Bodhibhadra says there are two kinds of śamatha: śamatha that is focused externally and śamatha that is focused internally. The externally focused śamatha is the ordinary kind that focuses on a stone or other object, and the special kind of śamatha is the kind that focuses on a statue or image of the Buddha. The internally focused śamatha has two kinds—visualization of the body and visualization based on the body. Visualization of the body is like focusing on something in the body such as the breath or the subtle channels or light rays within the body or the feeling of bliss. There are many types of meditation instruction given by the masters, but one can classify them into either meditation with external objects or meditation without external objects.

The third kind of śamatha meditation is *resting in the essence.* After meditating on an external object, then an internal object, we meditate by just resting in the essence. The mind is not focused on anything, but rests in a completely stable and unwavering state. When we say "mind" we think of it as being just one thing, but the Buddha described mind as being a collection of six or sometimes eight different kinds of consciousness. However, the five sense consciousnesses consist of: visual consciousness, which perceives and experiences visual forms; auditory consciousness, which perceives sounds based on the ear; olfactory consciousness, which perceives smells and is based on the nose; taste consciousness, for taste based on the tongue; and bodily consciousness, which perceives touch and physical sensations.

These five sense consciousnesses are said to be nonconceptual. They just see, hear, smell, taste, and feel and are not involved with thoughts such as "This is good or bad." Tilopa, in his instructions to Nāropa, said that appearances do no harm, but attachment to them causes problems. The actual seeing and hearing of things does not harm meditation in any way because these consciousnesses are nonconceptual. What causes an obstacle to meditation is developing attachment to a form, sound, etc. So there is no need to eliminate these sensations in one's meditation.

In India before the Buddha it was taught that there was just one consciousness. The example for how this one consciousness works is an example of a house with five or six windows and a monkey inside. The monkey would sometimes look out one window, then look out another window, so that on the outside it would appear as if there were different monkeys at different windows. But all the time it was just one monkey. The philosophers said that the house was like the mind and the windows were like the different sensory consciousnesses, and there was just one consciousness just as there was just one monkey. But the Buddha said there wasn't just one consciousness because if there were, then when one was seeing something, one wouldn't be able to hear a sound, or if one heard a sound, one wouldn't be able to smell, and so on. But in fact, one can see, hear, taste, smell, and feel physical sensations at the same time. So there are five distinct consciousnesses, not just one.

When one meditates, one does not use any of the five nonconceptual consciousnesses that are used to experience a sight, sound, smell, taste, or body sensation. In meditation only two mental consciousnesses are involved, and these are the unstable and stable mental consciousnesses. In the unstable consciousness (often called the mental consciousness) all kinds of thoughts arise and at times one feels attraction and happiness, other times dislike and unhappiness, and so on. This is our normal consciousness. Then there is the stable consciousness that remains completely unaffected by good or bad thoughts, pleasant or unpleasant experiences. The clarity of stable consciousness remains the same morning, noon, and night and is also called the ground consciousness, or *ālaya* consciousness. There is a third mental consciousness called afflicted consciousness that has no clarity and is in the state of delusion of always having the thought or feeling of "I." This thought of ego is always present whether the mind is distracted or not. It is a very subtle clinging to the self and one has it all the time whether one is aware of it or not, even when one is sleeping. Whatever one is doing, this subtle ego-clinging is always present, this thought of a "me." If one hears a sound, there is the subtle reaction, "Oh, this is dangerous to me." So, it is present all the time and until the attainment of the state of an arhat or of Buddhahood, all beings have this subtle ego-clinging. It is therefore called the lasting consciousness because the five sensory consciousnesses change continually. In all there are five sensory consciousnesses and three mental consciousnesses to make a total of eight.

One meditates with the sixth consciousness, called the mental consciousness because this consciousness deals with concepts. It is involved with the past, present, and future; good and bad; all the different kleśas; and so

35

on. The root of all these is mental consciousness, so this sixth consciousness is the root of all thoughts and concepts. In meditation one controls this consciousness that experiences all thoughts, delusions, and feelings. In meditation one controls it so that it stays still and these types of thoughts do not arise. This mental consciousness has two aspects: knowledge of other and knowledge of oneself. The knowledge of other occurs when the mind turns outward and thinks, "Oh, this is good or this is bad. I need this or I don't need this." Externally oriented knowledge is conceptual. The knowledge of oneself is very direct knowledge of what one is thinking. This self-awareness is nonconceptual; without this self-awareness, one wouldn't know what one is thinking about. It is a mindfulness that gives us clear knowledge of whether one is meditating or not. So in meditation there is this mindfulness and awareness.

When one is meditating, the mind or the general mental consciousness is being absorbed into the ground consciousness. For example, if one thinks of waves as thoughts and ground consciousness as the ocean, then the waves originate from the ocean and then merge or disappear into the ocean. In the same way, thoughts arise from the unceasing, unimpaired clarity of ground consciousness and then merge and disappear into ground consciousness. Also, when it is windy, the waves in the ocean increase; when it is calm, the waves subside and the ocean becomes stable and calm. In the same way, thoughts appear in the mind that are like a wind coming from the ground consciousness. This causes all the movement of thoughts in the mind. So if this wind from the ground consciousness subsides and merges into itself, the thoughts subside and the mind becomes still. This is described by Milarepa in one of his songs in which he talks about the manifestations of the mind in the same way that the waves are a manifestation of the sea. These waves come to rest in the sea just as thoughts come to rest in the mind. So thoughts are just the play or manifestation of the mind. Therefore, thoughts arise from the mind because they come from the mind. So when the wind arising from the ground consciousness is stilled, the mind becomes still.

So the ultimate form of śamatha is having thoughts disappear into the ground consciousness with the mind becoming stable and very relaxed. In other words, one has a great number of thoughts coming out of this ground consciousness and in meditation there is increased effort to absorb these thoughts back into the unceasing and unchanging clarity of ground consciousness. In such a way one will have a relaxed and still mind.

The sixth consciousness has to relax into the ground consciousness because it arises out of the ground consciousness and therefore must return to it. In meditation one needs the sixth consciousness to become still and calm without any thoughts arising. The ground consciousness in itself does not create an obstacle to meditation. But the seventh, or afflicted, consciousness is characterized by ego-clinging. It is always there. It does not create an obstacle to meditation but it does create an obstacle to liberation. Nevertheless, as one gradually becomes more accustomed to the realization of selflessness, this afflicted consciousness, this subtle ego-clinging gradually disappears. If the sixth mental consciousness becomes involved in the five sense consciousnesses, then it becomes an obstacle to meditation. But if the mind rests calmly and stably in itself and does not become involved in sense perceptions, then the sense perceptions do not create an obstacle to meditation. However, since the ordinary mind is habituated to involvement with sense perceptions, it is better for the beginner to practice in a quiet, isolated place.

3

IDENTIFYING EXPERIENCES IN ŚAMATHA MEDITATION

I N the *Treasury of Knowledge* the practice of meditation is described in terms of the textual tradition and also in terms of the oral instructions of the great meditators. The texts are important because they describe and explain the meaning of the teachings of the Buddha, and the instructions are important because they come from the actual experience of meditating. First, let us begin with the textual tradition that describes meditation in terms of the five things that can cause meditation to go wrong and the eight ways to eliminate these faults.

The Five Faults

When meditating, one has to recognize which experiences come out of meditation and which faults have to be eliminated. There are five faults that have to be eliminated through eight kinds of actions or antidotes. These five faults or defects prevent the development of meditation and are described by Asaṅga in the teachings of Maitreya in the *Differentiation of the Middle Way from the Extremes*. This text says that if the mind can rest on an object, then the mind becomes workable and very stable so we can do whatever we wish with the mind. In contrast, our normal mind is like riding a wild horse; when we are on a wild horse we cannot stay in one spot and we cannot go where we want to go. But if the mind becomes tame and workable, we can do whatever we want. We can use our mind to increase our wisdom and understanding, or if we need miraculous powers and clairvoyance, we can develop these. The way to obtain a workable mind is through eliminating the five faults to meditation.

The first fault is *laziness*. Laziness prevents the application of meditation because one doesn't even begin after receiving instructions in meditation. There are actually three kinds of laziness. First is lethargy, in which one isn't interested in doing anything except sleeping. Second is attachment to worldly activity resulting in no desire for dharma practice or meditation. Instead one devotes oneself to worldly activities such as hunting animals, lying and deceiving others, and so on. These are activities one enjoys, one is used to, or thinks about a lot. In one sense one has diligence, but it is an obstacle to practicing the dharma. This is also called attachment to negative activity. The third is despondency and self-accusation, which result in thinking, "Others can meditate, but I can't; others will understand the dharma, but I won't." The fact is that all beings are able to meditate and work on the path, but if they underestimate their capabilities, this is also called self-repudiation.

The second fault is *forgetting the instructions,* which is a lack of mindfulness on how to meditate properly. While meditating, one should be very clear about what one is doing, what faults must be eliminated, and what remedies must be applied. So one needs to remember the instructions for meditation.

The third fault is the *obstacle of stupor and agitation*. These are classified as a single fault. In stupor the mind is cloudy and dull. In its obvious form there is a loss of clarity of mind. In its subtle form there is some clarity, but it is very weak. There are also two kinds of agitation. There is an obvious kind in which one keeps thinking about what one has done or what fun one has had, so one is unable to rest the mind upon anything. In its subtle form one has apparent stability of mind, but there are still subtle thoughts that keep coming up. So there are two kinds of stupor and two kinds of agitation that cause an obstacle during meditation by causing the mind to lose its clarity and stability.

The fourth fault is *underapplication,* which occurs when dullness or agitation appear in one's meditation and one recognizes these thoughts, but doesn't apply a remedy. If one does not apply the remedy, meditation will not develop.

The fifth fault is *overapplication*. For example, dullness or agitation may appear in one's meditation, the remedy is applied, and the dullness or agitation is eliminated. Yet one continues to apply the remedy even though it is no longer useful. This is the fault of overapplication. The remedies should be used only when agitation and dullness appear; when they are eliminated, one should just rest in equanimity.

Although dullness and agitation have their individual characteristics, their effects as an obstacle to meditation are the same so they can be counted as just one fault. This system yields five faults, whereas if one counts these as separate, one gets six faults, which is the system used in the *Stages of Meditation* by Kamalaśīla.

The Eight Antidotes

To develop one's meditation, one has to eliminate the five faults. First one must be able to recognize what these faults are, then one needs to apply the remedies that eliminate them. These remedies are called the eight remedies that eliminate the five faults.

As described before, there are eight consciousnesses and these eight are called the principal mind. Within these consciousnesses occur transformations or changes. These changes are called mental events that can be sometimes good and sometimes bad. These mental events can also be described in terms of the five aggregates. There are the aggregates of form, sensation, identification, mental events, and consciousness. These describe the changes that occur within the principal mind. In the analysis of the aggregate of mental events, there are fifty-one different kinds of mental events such as laziness, forgetting instructions, and so on. These five faults are mental events, and the eight antidotes are also among this list of fifty-one mental events.

The first fault mentioned was laziness, a particularly powerful obstacle to meditation. There are four mental events that remedy this laziness. The first of these remedies is having aspiration or interest in meditation, meaning that one likes to meditate and is happy meditating. One could say that one is attached to meditation, but this attachment is positive, so we use the word *aspiration* because the attachment is to something that is negative and harmful. In Tibetan there are two words for "attachment"—*chagpa,* which is negative attachment usually translated as "attachment," and *möpa,* which is positive attachment usually translated as "aspiration." If someone likes stealing, then they are attached to stealing and this is *chagpa*—negative attachment. If someone wants to help someone else or wants to practice the dharma and they are attached to that, then this is *möpa* because it is beneficial to oneself and others. The meaning of these words appears to be the same in that one is thinking, "I have to do this" but with *möpa* one wants to help and with *chagpa* one wants to harm. The word *chagpa* also has the meaning of "being stuck" so that one stays where one is and can't go any higher. So this word means a block to one's development. If this attachment were something positive like meditation, then it would bring a positive result. If one likes meditating, then one will meditate, which will naturally eliminate the laziness as an obstacle. Sometimes, however, attachment is not positive and will not bring any benefit. For example, I received a letter from South Africa in which the person said that she liked her cat very much and then she lost her cat. It was a very beautiful cat, but the person was always thinking about the cat and couldn't forget it. This is an example of attachment that is not beneficial. What one needs is attachment to something that is beneficial, which we can call "aspiration."

The second remedy is zeal. If one has interest and motivation to practice, then one doesn't have to force oneself to practice meditation; there will be a natural zeal to practice.

The third remedy for laziness is faith. Although this is similar to the first remedy, aspiration means that one has something to aspire to, while faith means a belief in something very valuable.

The fourth remedy is literally called "well trained" and is also translated as "flexible" or "supple." This means that one's mind is ready at any moment to meditate. One doesn't have to think, "Oh, now I'm going to have to meditate—how difficult, what a strain meditation is." Without this suppleness of the "well-trained" mind and body, one does not have true śama-tha, but just a one-pointed state of mind. We can force our mind to be one-pointed with effort, but when we have the suppleness of meditation, the mind naturally rests one-pointedly without effort. This remedy and the previous three will eliminate the defect of laziness.

The fifth remedy is mindfulness, which remedies forgetting the instructions of meditation. One has a meditative state in which one doesn't forget the instructions. Mindfulness has three characteristics. First, one has a sharpness and clearness of mind in which the instructions are not forgotten. Second, although the mind is very sharp and focused, there are not many thoughts arising because meditation is nonconceptual, so there are not many thoughts arising and the mind is naturally focused one-pointedly on an object. Third, because one has trust and faith and has the suppleness or flexibility of having become well trained, meditation becomes pleasant with a sense of comfort and pleasure. These three qualities in one's meditation cause the meditation instructions not to be forgotten.

The third fault is stupor or agitation. First, one must recognize that agitation or stupor is appearing while meditating. When one finds either of these present, then one should apply a remedy to it. There are three methods to eliminate stupor or agitation. First, when one experiences stupor, one can visualize in one's heart a four-petaled white lotus with a white sphere in its center. Then imagine this going up to the crown of the head to the level of the hair and then to a distance of four finger-widths above the head. When there is agitation or too many thoughts, visualize an upside-down four-petaled black lotus in the heart with a little black sphere in its center. Imagine it going down to the level of one's seat and four finger-widths below that into the ground. A second remedy for stupor is to keep one's eyes wide open and look upward and tense one's body. For removing agitation one looks downward with eyes half closed, and relaxes the body. The third remedy for dullness is to be in a bright place. One opens all the windows and makes the room bright and cool and also wears light clothing. For agitation the room should be warm and darkened and one should wear thick clothing.

The fourth fault is inactivity in which one experiences dullness or agitation in one's meditation but does nothing about it. When this happens, one will fall under its power and obviously not be able to work toward enlightenment. When one recognizes that there is dullness or agitation during meditation, one should remember and apply the remedies with diligence. So performing the proper remedy will eliminate the defect of inactivity.

The fifth fault is the defect of overactivity, which means that when one is meditating with none of the five faults, one shouldn't do anything but rest in that meditative state. Doing this will eliminate the defect of overactivity.

In summary, there are eight mental remedies that can eliminate the five faults.

The Six Powers, Nine Levels, and Four Engagements

In the *Treasury of Knowledge* two different kinds of teachings are given from two different traditions. The first is the śamatha instruction in the textual tradition, which comes from the great scholars and siddhas of the past who composed texts on the instructions for meditation in words that are easy to understand. The second kind is the śamatha instructions from the practice tradition, which comes from siddhas describing the experience that comes from meditation and how one eliminates the faults and develops the good qualities of meditation. What follows is meditation from the textual tradition.

There are six powers that eliminate defects in śamatha meditation and bring about mental stability. The six powers bring about nine levels of mental stability. These nine levels of mental stability are created by six powers and four kinds of mental engagements.

The first of the six powers is the strength of the *power of listening,* or hearing, or receiving the teachings. This develops the first stage of mental stability or śamatha, which is called the settling or resting of the mind. Normally one's mind is distracted by thoughts, so one has to settle the mind a little in order not to be too distracted by external things. This is done through the power of listening. One hears the teachings of the Buddha, the teachings in the commentaries, and the explanations given by the scholars and siddhas. Through these one understands what meditation is like.

Hearing these, one is able to understand settling the mind and learns how to meditate. Marpa said that hearing and contemplating the teachings is like a torch that illuminates the darkness because if one has this source of light, one can see where one is going, what is there, and what might be dangerous and harmful. In Tibet, there is also a saying, "If one does not have a lamp and walks in the dark, then one's head might connect with a pillar." In the same way hearing and contemplating the teachings is like a lamp—it dispels the darkness and one sees what it is one must do and how one has to do it.

The second power is the *power of contemplation* or reflection, which means that one goes through the reason and the logic of the teachings to complete the continuity of teachings. With this power one develops the second stage of mental stability, which is called continued settlement. In the first stage one can rest the mind briefly, say for five minutes, and in the second stage one can do it longer, say for ten minutes.[7] These first two stages of listening to the teachings and continually contemplating them are the first two powers and accomplish the first mental engagement, which is called disciplined or controlled engagement. This first engagement involves the powers of hearing the teachings and contemplating them. In this first mental engagement the mind is controlled and focused with discipline.

The third power is the *power of mindfulness*. This is similar to the remedy for not forgetting one's meditation instructions discussed above. This power of mindfulness develops the third level of mental stability called the reestablished settlement. This means that when one is meditating, thoughts will arise and one becomes aware that one has become distracted by them. One returns to the state of meditation, so one reapplies oneself to it, reestablishing this settling in meditation. When there is a distraction that takes one away from resting in meditation, one is able to return to one's state of meditation repeatedly. This is reapplying a state of settling the mind. This power comes from the power of mindfulness because one becomes aware of the mind being distracted by some thought. With mindfulness one thinks, "I'm not going to be fully under the influence of this distracting thought" and mentally returns to what one is doing. This power of mindfulness also develops the fourth stage of mental stability, called intensified settlement, in which the mind that has been broadly focused is now focused very narrowly. The mind, for example, is narrowly focused on an object. The purpose of this kind of meditation is to focus the mind on something very subtle.

What can we do to prevent this continuous arising of thoughts? The text says that the mind is very vast and thoughts continuously arise and go everywhere. The mind has to be drawn inward and made more narrow, more constricted. So this is the state called the concentrated or intensified settlement, which is the fourth stage of śamatha meditation. The power necessary for this is the third power of mindfulness and memory. We need to remember teachings given by the Buddha, the commentaries, and the actual meditation instructions. We also need to be mindful of distractions so that when we become distracted we know this state allows us not to become attached or involved with that thought, so we can leave it and return to resting in meditation. Sometimes when we are meditating and a thought arises, we think, "This is an important thought. This one I really have to think about!" Since we spend such a short time in meditation, we should tell ourselves that we can think about the thought all the rest of the day when the meditation session is over.

Śāntideva gives an example of why it is necessary to have mindfulness. He says that thoughts and kleśas are like robbers or thieves because a thief will look at the person to see whether that person is strong or powerful. If he thinks he is not strong, he will rob him. If a thief believes someone is strong and has weapons and lots of reinforcement, the thief will not steal from him. In the same way, if a meditator has mindfulness and awareness, then he won't lose his meditation or practice of good actions. But, if someone does not have mindfulness and awareness, then thoughts and kleśas will arrive and steal away the meditation and destroy the practice of good actions. The remedy that prevents the attack of mind poisons and thoughts is having mindfulness and awareness.

The mind is like a door. Whatever comes in, whether it be a thief or a great deal of wealth, must come through that door. Similarly, if any negative or positive qualities come in, they come in through the mind. Likewise, if one goes into a bank, for example, there is normally a guard at the door with a gun to prevent thieves from entering. In the same way, the mind is like a door and one needs mindfulness as a guard present all the time. Just as a guard is not enough, one needs the weapon of awareness. If mindfulness and awareness are there all the time, then the thoughts and kleśas won't be able to come in and steal what is positive. To carry the example further, Indian banks put a guard with a gun to guard the door. But since they are afraid that there is nothing to keep the guard from robbing the bank, their solution is to chain the guard to a pillar outside. So Indian banks have a guard with a rifle chained to a pillar to stop thieves from coming in and the guard from robbing the bank. In the same way, to protect one's meditation one needs to have mindfulness guarding the door of the mind and in order to prevent the mindfulness from losing control, one chains it there with awareness.

The fourth power is the *power of awareness,* which means one knows exactly what is occurring and what one is doing. Normally, one isn't aware of what is happening, but this power of awareness develops two levels of mental stability, namely, the fifth level called taming and the sixth level called pacification. Normally, our mind cannot be motivated to meditate and so it is very difficult to meditate. With the power of taming, however, we become aware of the qualities and benefits of meditating: that it benefits ourselves and others; that this meditation can help us develop clairvoyance and miraculous powers and increase our understanding and wisdom. Being aware of all the qualities that result from meditation will cause us to be attracted to meditation and encourage us to meditate so our mind becomes tamed. Thus this power of awareness that develops the level of taming leads to the sixth level of mental stability called pacification. After śamatha meditation what is important in the postmeditation state is mindfulness and awareness. With mindfulness we don't forget the condition of our mind and with awareness we are very clear about what is happening all the time. To those who want to control their mind, Śāntideva said, "I ask with hands clasped together to make mindfulness and awareness very important." During meditation sessions, mindfulness and awareness are also important, and after meditation sessions one should maintain mindfulness and awareness as much as possible.

In Tibetan *drenpa* means "mindfulness," and *sheshin* means "awareness." *Drenpa* also means "mindfulness and memory." It means that one is mindful of what one is doing and remembers what one has to do whether one is meditating, whether one has lost the power of concentration, and so on. Mindfulness is like a causal condition and awareness is like the result. If one has very concentrated mindfulness, one immediately notices a thought arising and this becomes awareness, which becomes sheshin, and one knows what is occurring. Normally, one does not know what is in one's mind or what one is thinking, so there is no awareness. But if one has mindfulness, then it is said to the extent that mindfulness brings mental stability, one has awareness. So when one has mindfulness, it is through one's awareness of what is happening.

At this level of pacification we become aware of the negative qualities of distraction. Śāntideva explains this by saying that when the mind is distracted, it is between the fangs of the wild animal of the kleśas, and from mental distractions come all the difficulties and mental hardships of this and future lives. Being in a state of distraction will increase the negative qualities of the mind more and more. However, being aware of the negative qualities motivates us to meditate.

The fifth power is the *power of diligence*. This power creates the seventh level of mental stability, which is complete pacification. In the previous level of pacification one contemplates the qualities of meditation and the faults of distraction and eliminates these. Sometimes, however, with very strong obstacles such as unhappiness, regret, or aggression, just thinking of the good qualities of meditation will not eliminate them right away. Instead, one needs the power of diligence so that one can eliminate all strong obstacles such as attachment, aggression, and ignorance and can create the seventh level of meditative stability of complete pacification.

The power of diligence also creates the eighth level of mental stability, which is called one-pointedness because all powerful distractions of mind have been eliminated and the mind can rest one-pointedly. At the level of one-pointedness one can meditate without much effort, and this power of diligence is used to maintain this one-pointed state.

The first mental engagement is called the tightly controlled engagement and is associated with the first two levels of mental stability. The second mental engagement, called interrupted engagement, is associated with the third through seventh levels of stability. Interrupted engagement means that one rests the mind in a state of stability; then it is interrupted by some defect and one then applies the remedy. One continues this repeatedly so that one's stability is continually interrupted. At the level of the eighth mental stability of one-pointedness one develops the third mental engagement called the uninterrupted mental engagement. At this point the mind focuses on one point and remains there without interruption.

The sixth power is the *power of familiarization*. At this level the mind is naturally settled without the need for effort or discipline. The fourth mental engagement associated with this power is the naturally present mental engagement. The ninth level of mental stability is called resting in equanimity. So at the ninth level of mental stability with the sixth power and the fourth mental engagement, the mind just rests in equanimity, relaxed without effort. This is the final stage of mental stability.

The five defects and eight remedies are taught in the *Differentiation of the Middle Way from the Extremes,* which is by Asaṅga and is one of the five works of Maitreya. The Buddha's teachings are divided into the sūtras, the vinaya, and the abhidharma. The *Differentiation of the Middle Way from the Extremes* is a commentary on the abhidharma. The nine levels of mental stability are taught in Maitreya's *Ornament of the Mahāyāna Sūtras* by Asaṅga. This text explains and clarifies the teachings of the sūtras. The six powers and four mental engagements are found in one of the five treatises of Asaṅga called the *Levels of the Śrāvakas.*

To summarize, when we meditate, faults arise that prevent us from developing our meditation (see table 1).

When the bodhisattvas meditated, they saw the faults that arose and then identified them and were able to find remedies that could eliminate these faults. But if we don't recognize these faults when meditating, we will not progress toward Buddhahood. Through the teachings we can identify these defects and know how to apply the correct remedy. This particular teaching is one that should be experienced directly, not just studied intellectually. As the five defects arise in our meditation, we should apply the eight remedies and use the six powers and the four mental engagements in our meditation. Also, through our meditation we should be able to identify which level of mental stability we have

Summary of the Powers, Levels,
and Engagements

POWER	LEVELS OF STABILITY	ENGAGEMENT
1. Hearing the teachings 2. Contemplating the teachings	1. Resting the mind 2. Resting in the mind longer	1. Tightly focused or controlled engagement
3. Memory or mindfulness	3. Continuously resettling the mind 4. Intensely settled mind	
4. Awareness	5. Taming the mind 6. Pacification of the mind	2. Interrupted mental engagement
5. Diligence	7. Complete pacification of the mind 8. One-pointed mind	3. Uninterrupted mental engagement
6. Familiarization	9. Resting in equanimity	4. Naturally settled engagement

reached. Therefore, these meditation instructions are very important and we need to understand them thoroughly.

The Tradition of Oral Instruction

The instruction of śamatha has been passed on orally from one individual to another. One first receives instruction on śamatha much like the instruction in this book. This first stage is called the *experience of instability*. When one begins to meditate, one first experiences the mind as very unstable with many, many thoughts arising. There are good thoughts and bad thoughts and this is likened to a waterfall rushing off a cliff. When the water hits the bottom, it splashes up with a great deal of agitation and makes many waves. In meditation it seems one has never had so many thoughts and one thinks, "I am getting worse because of my meditation." But, in fact, one is not developing more thoughts; rather, before one had begun to meditate, one didn't think about how many thoughts one had. One didn't analyze them and so one wasn't aware of the number of thoughts. Actually, meditation is the beginning of dealing with one's mind because one becomes aware of one's thoughts.

When we begin to meditate continually, we begin to have a second experience called the *experience of attainment*. With this experience we begin to feel that we have accomplished good meditation. This experience is likened to a mountain stream or a river in a gully. The river is still rough with many waves, but it isn't as powerful and fierce as a waterfall.

The next level of meditation becomes easier and is

likened to a slow-flowing river. The meditation is easier but not to the extent that it is a continuous state of meditative stability with no thoughts arising. But it is not as rough and unconnected as the second stage of attainment. So now there is a kind of smoothness and gentleness because the power of thoughts has decreased. This third level is called the *experience of familiarization*.

The fourth level is known as the *experience of stability* because there is a continuous state of stability without a flow of disturbing thoughts. At this stage one has reached the degree of stability in which one has control over one's mind. This is compared to an ocean that is calm and without waves.

The fifth level is called the *experience of complete stability* and is the final stage in which one is not disturbed by any kind of experience. The experiences that arise in this fifth level are bliss, clarity, and the absence of thoughts. For example, while meditating one might experience a great sensation of bliss and later this bliss disappears. Or one day suddenly a great clarity arises in one's meditation and one might think, "What is this clarity I'm experiencing?" Or one might experience a state devoid of conceptual thoughts. These are the three kinds of experiences that can arise in śamatha meditation. At this level whatever arises does not affect one's mental stability and one is unaffected by conditions such as those that create craving or anger or even love and compassion. As a result one develops great clarity and brightness of mind that is devoid of dullness or stupidity. The example for this experience is a candle flame burning in still air; it is very bright and gives good light, but if it is in moving air, it just gives intermittent light. Once the mind is stable and becomes unaffected by thoughts, then one is able to have a clear understanding of things. There are two aspects of this perfect understanding: the aspect of clarity and the aspect of purity. Clarity is when everything is seen with sharp vision, everything is understood very clearly, vividly, and in detail. The aspect of purity is when the mind is not stained by uncertainty and there is no fluctuation in this clarity. It is completely pure and unpolluted understanding.

Normally, when we develop some mental stability and have a good meditative experience, we think, "This is wonderful, I must be becoming a siddha." When we have a bad meditative experience, on the other hand, we think, "This is terrible, I'm obviously doing everything wrong." But whatever experience occurs—good or bad—we should just continue meditating. If a good experience arises, we should not feel we are better than everyone else and feel proud; we should just continue meditating. If a bad experience arises, we should not become depressed because that will just cause us to fall into a lower existence; we should just proceed with our meditation and maintain the practice continually. When Gampopa had the experience of having the Hevajra maṇḍala appear before him or saw the whole Chakra-saṃvara maṇḍala or met his yidam deity in his meditation, he would go to his teacher Milarepa and ask him what it meant. Milarepa would always say it was nothing at all and that there was nothing good or bad in it and that he should go back and carry on meditating. Sometimes Gampopa would have very bad experiences while meditating. One time the whole world began to spin until he threw up; another time everything went completely dark so that Gampopa had to feel his way around on his hands and knees and thought this must have been caused by a demon. Still another time he heard a loud shouting from nowhere and thought that he had gone insane. When he went and asked Milarepa about it, Milarepa just said it was nothing at all, not good or bad, and told him to just carry on meditating. Likewise, we should just carry on with our meditation whether we have good or bad experiences.

The Accomplishment of Śamatha

So far the nature of meditation in the scholastic and oral traditions has been discussed. Now let us discuss the result of meditation or the signs of accomplishment in meditation. The result of meditation is the experience of bliss of mind and body. This bliss of mind and body is called literally "well trained." In Tibetan it is *shinjang,* which is actually a description of the cause of the result; the name of the cause, "being well trained," is used for the actual result. So actually being well trained is the cause, but the name is given to the result. *Shintu* means "a great deal" or "very much" and *jangpa* means "trained" or the mastery of something. So *shintu jangpa* means that "one is well trained in something." The text says that if one has not attained this state of being well trained in body and mind, then one has not really reached the full attainment of śamatha meditation. Even if one has attained the highest (the fourth) mental engagement and the final (ninth) stage of mental stability, if one doesn't have the well-trained body and mind, one hasn't achieved full śamatha meditation. This is explained in the *Definite Explanation of the View.* In this sūtra Maitreya asks what the meditation of a bodhisattva is like when he or she has developed all the mental engagements, but still doesn't have a well-trained body and mind. Maitreya also asks if one has achieved śamatha meditation when one hasn't developed this well-trained body and mind. The Buddha answered, "No." So to have valid śamatha meditation one must be well trained so that the mind and body are completely workable and one has the one-pointed level of mental stability of the desire realm.

A description of this state is given by Asaṅga in his *Compendium of the Abhidharma.* He stated that one needs to attain this well-trained mind and body that cuts through the continuum of the factors that lead to negative states. If one can remove these negative propensities, then the mind becomes workable and usable. With meditation and this workability of mind one can eliminate all the obscurations of the kleśas. Asaṅga then goes on to describe these negative propensities of body and mind. The negative propensity of the body is to resist involvement in good actions and meditation so that a great deal of effort is needed to do these things. The negative propensity of the mind makes meditation difficult so that the mind cannot rest naturally or easily in meditation. Negative propensities of the body result in a slight resistance to doing positive actions, and one feels physically very heavy and uncomfortable when meditating. First, one develops mental suppleness in which the mind becomes stable, pleasant, and relaxed. Then one develops physical suppleness because when the mind becomes very comfortable and still, then the life air (Skt. *prāṇa*) becomes unobstructed and undisturbed so it permeates the body. With this flow of life air the body feels very light and comfortable and the negative propensities of the body are eliminated. This feeling is not just mental, but is an actual physical sensation.

How do these physical and mental sensations of śamatha occur? This question is answered in Asaṅga's *Levels of the Śrāvakas*. First, one experiences a very subtle sensation and one doesn't know if it is in the body or mind. One just feels a very subtle, pleasant sensation. Later on it becomes stronger and more obvious and one knows it is a definite pleasurable sensation. Still later on it becomes very strong and one experiences bliss and comfort. One becomes very confident of one's meditation at this point, but one should not become attached to or proud of this sensation and think that it is special. Instead, one should remain in a state of equanimity and think, "This sensation can come or go, but it doesn't matter." If one can rest at this time in equanimity, then one can achieve a very deep state of peace. This bliss is said to be like a shadow because when a shadow appears it is definitely there; but it has no substance. In the same way when this experience of bliss is present, it is definitely there, but it has no substance. One shouldn't cling to this sensation of pleasure or one will fall under its power.

When one has fully attained a well-trained mind and body, then there is no external or internal distraction or disturbance and the mind is completely stable. At this level all the obvious kleśas are eliminated and pacified. If one has fully developed a well-trained body and mind, then one's meditation will be an experience of bliss. If this well-trained state is strong, one experiences these sensations before, during, and after meditation as well. The power of this well-trained state creates a great clarity of perception so that one sees everything down to the smallest detail—down to the smallest particles. In fact, there are three particular qualities of a well-trained mind and body—the sensation of bliss, great clarity of perception, and the disappearance of the sensation of the ten characteristics. The ten characteristics are the sensory sensations of vision, sound, smell, taste, and bodily sensation; the time perception of past, present, and future; and the gender perception of masculine and feminine. When resting in meditation, it is as if one has blended with space and there is no conception of these ten qualities, as if everything has disappeared. Then after the meditation session, it is as if the body suddenly reappears.

The Purpose of Accomplishing Śamatha

In the sūtras and the tantras it is said that śamatha is the basis for all meditation. All meditative states, including vipaśyanā, come from and depend on the development of śamatha. For example, if one wants to grow plants, one must have good soil, and if one has good soil one doesn't need to put a lot of effort into gardening because the plants will grow quickly and easily in good soil. However, with poor soil, no matter how much effort one puts into gardening, one cannot grow good plants. In the same way, if one has good śamatha, then one can easily develop clairvoyant and miraculous powers, vipaśyanā, and wisdom. Good śamatha meditation will also diminish all the negativities of the mind by creating a state of peace. Then no matter what physical pain, hardships, or mental obstacles and confusion occur, the suffering does not harm one because all these things are suppressed and diminished by mental stability.

Kamalaśīla in the first book of his *Stages of Meditation* says that if one is able to rest in a state of equanimity, one is able to gain an understanding of the true nature of things. The Buddha also gained his attainments by resting in this state of equanimity. If one cannot rest in equanimity, one will not gain the understanding of the true nature of phenomena. The mind will be like a bird's feather blown in the wind, unable to stay in one place.

PART TWO

INSIGHT
[lhag mthong]

4

VIPAŚYANĀ: INSIGHT
MEDITATION

THE explanation of vipaśyanā, or insight meditation, is divided into five parts. These are the
prerequisite conditions for vipaśyanā, the different forms of vipaśyanā, the categorizations of the nature
of vipaśyanā, the methods of meditation, and the mea-
sure of accomplishment. The first section deals with
the conditions necessary for vipaśyanā meditation.
Kamalaśīla in his second book of the *Stages of Meditation* describes three conditions necessary to develop
vipaśyanā.

The Prerequisites for Practicing Vipaśyanā

First of all one needs to learn how to develop vipaśyanā
meditation because one doesn't naturally possess this
knowledge. Therefore, one must rely on a pure being
to give dharma teachings, and this being should be very
learned and have studied and understood the texts and
the commentaries on the Buddha's teachings. It should
be someone with actual experience of the teachings and
someone who in his or her compassion will take care of
the pupil. In this age there are many dharma books and
many people read them and meditate according to what
they have read. This leads to various difficulties such as

finding their bodies shaking or working very hard without getting any signs of accomplishment from their meditation. One really needs to depend on a special and learned teacher because a book cannot adapt the instruction to one's own nature and capabilities. Therefore, one needs to rely on a special being who is able to teach in accordance with one's specific abilities.

There are different kinds of teachers. Some are very scholarly and give thorough explanations based on the commentaries on various texts. Others may not be very scholarly but give instructions based on a great deal of personal experience of meditation so he or she can explain what will happen in meditation. There is also what is called the old lady's pointing instruction. This is like an instruction from an old lady who really doesn't know very much, but is able to point out the key things to look for. The commentaries on meditation do not give points on the direct experience of meditation or these "pointing out" instructions. It is therefore important for meditators to receive direct instruction from an experienced teacher.

The benefits of a genuine teacher come not just from being with and having conversations with the teacher, but from receiving instructions that are beneficial to one's progress. A genuine teacher also gives the actual teachings of the Buddha or the experiences of the bodhisattvas and great siddhas, and not teachings of his own personal creation. The teachings that are the most beneficial are those that come from a pure or genuine text, that is, the actual teachings *(sūtras)* of the Buddha or the commentaries *(śāstras),* which come from the great bodhisattvas or the great siddhas. The teacher should be able to read and understand these teachings and be able to pass them on to his or her pupils. Therefore, one should receive the teachings from one's teacher and contemplate them so that one develops an understanding of them. The second point, then, is that one must receive teachings from the teacher.

In general, Buddhist practice involves the correct view, meditation, and proper conduct. With the correct view we are able to meditate and through meditation we develop proper conduct. Therefore the root of these is the view. To develop the correct view, we don't just receive these teachings, but rather we must analyze and examine them continuously. We shouldn't accept teachings with blind faith, however, but we should analyze and examine them so that we can cut through our uncertainty and doubt that the teachings from our teacher are correct and will lead us on the path. From this develops a definite view that the teacher's instructions are genuine, and this is called the definitive or correct viewpoint. Correct viewpoint is the principal causal condition for vipaśyanā. These three aspects of depending on a teacher, receiving the teachings, and analyzing them develop the correct view of vipaśyanā.

To develop the correct viewpoint, we must rely not on the provisional meaning, but on the definitive meaning. Provisional meanings are teachings given by the Buddha to persons of lesser capabilities who were not able to believe or grasp the actual teachings. The definitive meanings are those that describe things as they actually are. To have a genuine view one must depend on the definitive meaning. One has to recognize directly what is the true meaning of phenomena and distinguish it from the provisional meaning. When the teachings of the vajrayāna were transmitted to Tibet, the practice of contemplating the teachings by relying on the commentaries was developed. Some Chinese and some Western scholars state that this is a defect in the Tibetan Buddhist tradition because it relies so heavily on commentaries instead of relying on the actual words of the Buddha. The reliance on commentaries, however, has a very special purpose because when the Buddha gave teachings, he gave particular teachings to various individuals according to their particular nature so that some of his teachings were the provisional truths and some were the definitive truths.

If one has to go through the Buddha's teachings deciding which teachings are provisional and which are definitive with logical analysis, one could make many mistakes. But the Buddha prophesied that various masters would come in the future and write commentaries on the teachings to show which teachings are provisional and which definitive. In particular, the *Treasury of Knowledge* mentions two long, pure traditions: the tradition of Nāgārjuna who founded the tradition of the profound view, and the tradition of Asaṅga who founded the tradition of vast conduct. These two great masters were able to clearly distinguish the provisional and definitive teachings of the Buddha with their commentaries. One should rely on the commentaries of these two great masters not only for differentiating between these two meanings, but also for their vast content. The *Prajñāpāramitā* teachings, for example, contain twelve volumes, and it would be difficult to go through these deciding the definitive and provisional meaning of each passage. Hence these commentaries summarize the vast teachings of the Buddha and give their real meanings. For example, Asaṅga in the *Orna-*

ment of Clear Realization condensed the *Prajñāpāramitā* into just twenty pages. There are also teachings of the Buddha that have obscure or hidden meanings or there are teachings that are very short and concise. So there are commentaries that elucidate and expand the meaning of these teachings in detail. For this reason commentaries are very important and their understanding is a necessary condition for the development of vipaśyanā.

The Different Forms of Vipaśyanā

There are four main forms of vipaśyanā. The first kind of vipaśyanā is the vipaśyanā of the Tirthika (non-Buddhist) traditions and is found primarily in India. These non-Buddhist traditions practice śamatha meditation to pacify and eliminate most of the obvious kleśas. The second kind of vipaśyanā is the vipaśyanā teachings the Buddha gave to the śrāvakas and pratyekabuddhas who could not understand the very profound or vast meaning. The third kind of vipaśyanā is the vipaśyanā of the bodhisattvas who follow the six pāramitās. These teachings are very profound and vast. The fourth kind of vipaśyanā is that which uses bliss as a special method for quickly attaining realization, or the vipaśyanā of the mantrayāna.

In the vipaśyanā of the Tirthika tradition, one contemplates the "peaceful and the coarse" aspects. For example, one might contemplate a coarse kleśa such as anger in one's meditation. One can realize that anger is harmful to oneself and others and that without anger the mind would be peaceful and happy. So it is easy to see the benefits of the absence of this obvious kleśa of anger, which is peace. So with this meditation one can then overcome anger. One may wonder if there is something wrong with this non-Buddhist form of vipaśyanā. Actually, there isn't anything wrong with this tradition, which is called the "common tradition" because it is common to Buddhists and non-Buddhists. In the Buddhist tradition this vipaśyanā is known as the worldly level of vipaśyanā because one recognizes the mind poisons and their faults and tries to make the mind still and stable. The practice is performed to calm the mind and subjugate the mind poisons rather than to understand emptiness or the absence of self. Calming the mind eliminates the faults on the level of the desire realm so that one can attain the first level of mental stability in the form realm.

The vipaśyanā of the śrāvakas and pratyekabuddhas (the solitary buddhas) is for those who are without the necessary fortitude to accomplish complete Buddhahood. These two kinds of realized beings, the śrāvakas and the pratyekabuddas, are found within the hīnayāna tradition. The difference between them is the accumulation of merit. If there is some accumulation of merit, then one is a śrāvaka; if there is a great accumulation of merit, then one is a pratyekabuddha. However, in terms of śamatha and vipaśyanā meditation there is only a slight difference between them because both meditate on the four noble truths. The practice of śrāvakas and pratyekabuddhas is based on the four noble truths, which are divided into sixteen aspects (see table 2). With this type of vipaśyanā, peace is based on the four noble truths as a description of saṃsāra and nirvāṇa. The first noble truth is a description of saṃsāra, which is called the truth of suffering. The second truth of origination looks at the cause of saṃsāra, which originates from

The Sixteen Aspects of the Four Noble Truths

THE TRUTH OF SUFFERING
(*Duḥkhasatya*)

Suffering	(*duḥkha*)
Impermanence	(*anitya*)
Emptiness	(*śūnyatā*)
Selflessness	(*anātmaka*)

THE TRUTH OF ORIGIN
(*Samudayasatya*)

Origin	(*samudaya*)
Strong production	(*prabhava*)
Cause	(*hetu*)
Condition	(*pratyaya*)

THE TRUTH OF CESSATION
(*Nirodhasatya*)

Cessation	(*nirodha*)
Pacification	(*śānta*)
Excellence	(*praṇīta*)
Definite emergence	(*niḥsaraṇa*)

THE TRUTH OF THE PATH
(*Mārgasatya*)

Path	(*mārga*)
Suitability	(*nyāya*)
Achievement	(*pratipatti*)
Deliverance	(*nairyāṇika*)

karma and the kleśas. The third truth of cessation occurs if karma and the kleśas are eliminated and this results in nirvāṇa. The fourth truth is following and practicing the truth of the path. In the vipaśyanā of śrāvakas and pratyekabuddhas the actual nature of these four truths has to be understood along with their subcategories. The truth of suffering is divided into impermanence, suffering, absence of self, and emptiness. The truth of origination, the truth of cessation, and the truth of the path are also divided into four parts, making a total of sixteen subdivisions.

What are the four noble truths? There is saṃsāra, from which one seeks to gain liberation, and there is nirvāṇa, which one seeks to attain. One wishes to attain liberation from saṃsāra, the nature of which is suffering. So the first truth of suffering is that one wishes to attain liberation from the suffering of saṃsāra. One wishes to attain nirvāṇa, and this is the third truth of cessation. However, one cannot simply say one wants to attain liberation and achieve it. This is because all phenomena arise from causes, so saṃsāra and nirvāṇa also arise from a cause. This cause is the second truth of origination, which is karma and the kleśas. Therefore, one needs to eliminate the cause of saṃsāra, which is karma and the mind poisons. When these are eliminated, one has attained freedom from the truth of suffering, from saṃsāra. To be able to attain freedom from the truth of suffering and saṃsāra, one must be able to eliminate the origin of suffering. One can't eliminate karma and the kleśas directly because their source is ego-clinging that has to be eliminated. The way to eliminate this is the fourth noble truth of path which is the meditation on selflessness, that is, to meditate on the five aggregates and one's association of the idea of "self" or "mine" to these five aggregates. Through realization of selflessness, one can eliminate the clinging to a self, and the mind poisons will naturally subside. When these subside, one will be able to practice the path, which is the fourth truth, and finally attain the truth of cessation.

In the vipaśyanā of the Tirthikas there is the partial elimination of the obvious mental negativities, but they are not completely eliminated. In the vipaśyanā of the śrāvakas the cause of the kleśas is identified as the clinging to the idea of self or of "I" or "mine." A belief in a self is a delusion because actually there is no self or things that belong to a self. When one is able to realize the absence of self in vipaśyanā meditation, then the natural clinging to self just vanishes. So the main meditation of the śrāvakas is the meditation on the absence of self. An example of this ego-clinging happened to me the other day when I noticed that one of the links in the metal strap of my watch was broken. When I saw that, I thought, "Oh no, the strap might break and I will lose my watch!" I was worried even though only a tiny bit of metal was missing. When one examines the watch, one cannot find any "mine" associated with the watch—it was made in a factory and it is just a piece of metal that didn't originate from me in any way. If I were without the delusion of "my" associated with the watch, I wouldn't have experienced the discomfort and suffering of seeing the broken link.

A lot of people think that Buddhism is an unpleasant practice that makes us unhappy. Buddhism teaches the nature of suffering, the absence of self, and impermanence. We may think that to meditate on these can make

73

us uncomfortable, and make us lose our feeling of confidence and so on. Buddhism does teach these, but it is taught because we need this information to attain liberation from suffering. Once we understand the nature of suffering, we can be liberated from it. Through this understanding of the nature of suffering, our wisdom will also increase and develop.

Ordinary beings have an innate ego-clinging. This clinging to a self occurs in a child; no one needs to teach it. Animals also have this clinging to self. But what is this clinging? There is really no stable object for this clinging; it is a delusion. Sometimes one thinks this self is the mind. But when one examines the self more closely, one discovers that it is not in the hair, not in the bone, the eyes, the nose, the brain, and so on. One finds that these are only body parts with no self identified with them. One's body is just a physical aggregate of form and the self is nowhere to be found.

Perceiving the body as not being the self, one may think that the mind is the self. But the mind is just a succession of instants, like the flow of a river with each instant being a new instant of mind. There are thoughts one had yesterday, thoughts one has now, and thoughts one will have in the future. One may wonder if a previous thought will ever come back again. It does not come back. When one was a child, one had a child's mind; when one grows up and becomes old, the mind is different. The mind has different characteristics, different thoughts, a different process of thinking, and a different degree of understanding. Even the mind between yesterday and today is different. There is a continuous succession of different kinds of thoughts and states of mind. So one asks, "Is the self of today, the mind of

74

yesterday?" No, it is gone. Then, "Is the self of today, the mind of now?" No, because the mind of now is going to disappear, so that can't be one's self either. In a further analysis there is visual consciousness, auditory consciousness, mental consciousness, and so on. Even mental consciousness is a mixture of different things. There is the grasping at something that is red, a conception that something is white, etc., so the mental consciousness is an accumulation of different parts and therefore is not a single entity that one could say is one's self. Having understood the absence of a self, one meditates on selflessness and gains understanding of the four noble truths. Through this process one attains the vipaśyanā of the śrāvakas and pratyekabuddhas.

The meditation of vipaśyanā of the bodhisattva of the mahayāna path is the meditation on the selflessness of phenomena. A bodhisattva practices meditation based on the six pāramitās. There is the selflessness of the individual already discussed and the selflessness of phenomena. This second kind of selflessness is the realization that inner consciousness and external phenomena are naturally peaceful and empty. So the mahāyāna meditator believes that the root of saṃsāra is the kleśas and that the root of the kleśas is ego-clinging. Eliminating clinging to a self is the way to be liberated from saṃsāra.

To eliminate kleśas, the mahāyāna meditators meditate on the nature of external and internal phenomena in detail to discover that they are completely insubstantial, like bubbles in water. With this realization the kleśas naturally disappear. The belief in the reality of external phenomena is called the obscuration of knowledge, and when this obscuration is eliminated there is liberation from saṃsāra. The bodhisattvas therefore meditate on emptiness (śūnyatā). In the *Heart Sūtra* the Buddha says there are "no eyes, no ears, no nose, no tongue, [etc.]" and that there is "no form, no sound, no smell, no taste, [etc.]" One might interpret this as the Buddha saying there are literally no eyes, and so on. When the Buddha gave this teaching, he was explaining what one experiences when one rests in this state of samādhi meditation. He didn't explain this in the sūtra because at the time his pupils were in a meditative state and therefore were able to understand the teaching without explanation. The Buddha taught this way in the *Heart Sūtra* and the other *Prajñāpāramitā* sūtras. These teachings are explained in commentaries such as Chandrakīrti's *Entering into the Middle Way;* by examining cause and effect he demonstrates the nature of emptiness by examining the nature of cause. There is also Master Jñānagarbha who, in his *Differentiation of the Two Truths*, shows the nature of emptiness through the analysis of the effect. Then there is Nāgārjuna's *Knowledge of the Middle Way,* which demonstrates the emptiness of all phenomena.

In Tibet there are a number of great commentaries on emptiness, such as that of Lama Mipam, who described how the Indian master Śāntarakṣita came to Tibet and wrote the *Adornment of the Middle Way,* which explains emptiness in terms of things not being "one thing or many things." Mipam describes this approach as being very powerful and easy to understand. For example, for things to be real, they must be a single thing; let us say for a "hand" to exist it must be one thing: a hand. If one looks at it, one sees a hand; if one shows it to others, they agree it is a hand. However, examining it more closely, one sees that it is a thumb, a finger, skin, flesh and bones, and so on. So it is not a hand, but, as the Buddha said, it is just an aggregation of all sorts of parts that have come together. So the hand really is the appearance that arises from the interdependence of parts that we call a hand, but there is no real hand there. It is like this for all things, and using this logic, one becomes convinced of the nature of emptiness.

The vipaśyanā meditation of the mahāyāna is on the realization of emptiness, which is also called dependent origination. This means that all phenomena that arise have a dependence upon other phenomena and therefore no true existence of their own. For example, with the reflection of the moon on water, there is no real moon in the water, but due to the interdependence of the moon in the sky and the water on the ground, a reflection of the moon appears. Also, when one examines the water to see where the moon is, there isn't a single location where the moon's reflection is. In this same way, all phenomena originate through dependence upon something else and have no true existence of their own. The realization of this fact is the realization of emptiness, and with this realization, the kleśas cease. So to put an end to the kleśas, one meditates on emptiness.

Taking another example, if one takes a piece of paper and rips it up, the act doesn't upset anyone. But when one takes out a piece of paper that happens to be a ten-dollar bill and begins to rip it, the act suddenly becomes something important. Why is it suddenly important? It is important because everyone agrees that a ten-dollar bill is important, but in actual fact, it is just a piece of paper. Why is something made important by people?

There is no particular reason, it just happens that everyone thinks that it is important. So this is dependent origination—the value of various things is dependent on what everyone thinks. This is not only true with paper money; everyone thinks that gold is more valuable than iron. Why is gold more valuable? Simply because everyone thinks so. Gold itself does not have *amrita* flowing out of it; gold is just a metal. In this way, the mind clings to things; it perceives some things as good, other things as bad, but nothing is ultimately good or bad in itself. It is just a mental perception and the nature of things is emptiness.

Everything comes into being through interdependence. For example, if one has two pieces of paper, one that is small and one that is big, they are small and big because they depend on each other. If one puts a larger piece of paper next to them, then the big piece becomes the medium-sized piece. In itself it is not a big piece of paper or a small piece of paper. Large and small, good and bad, beautiful and ugly are all creations of the mind and do not have actual existence. There is a fable to illustrate this point. There was once a rabbit who was resting in the shade of a tree by the lake. Suddenly the wind broke off one of the branches of the tree and it fell into the water, making a big splash. This sound frightened the rabbit and without thinking he ran away. While running he encountered two mice. They asked him why he was running and the rabbit said, "There was a great sound back there." That frightened the mice and they began running as well. So, we are like the mice, we don't ask why a ten-dollar bill is valuable, we simply answer, "Well, everyone thinks so." Things don't have a natural existence of their own, but the mind just clings to them. So the story continues. While all the animals were running, they met a lion who asked them why they were running away. They answered that there was a terrible sound in the lake and the lion said, "Well, it was just a sound. Maybe we should investigate what the sound was before running away." Then they all went together to the lake and saw the branch floating in the water. Similarly, we are always thinking, "This is good, this is bad," and so on. If we analyze these thoughts and see that these things have no existence of their own, our mind can become peaceful without the kleśas and we can then gain freedom from delusion and realize the true nature of things.

For an example of dependent origination we may think, "I feel very happy in the environment. In other places, I get depressed and homesick." Through dependent origination we experience pleasant and unpleasant places. When we meditate, however, there are no thoughts of pleasant and unpleasant and we don't have thoughts of arriving at nice or unpleasant places. Instead, we have the realization of the sameness of all places and so we have a state of peace without the suffering involved in thinking we are in an undesirable place.

There is a story about Buddha's younger brother Nanda (not Ānanda who was his cousin) who had a wife called Puṇḍarīka whom he liked very much. The Buddha asked him to come and receive teachings, but Nanda never went because he was worried that these teachings would make him want to become a monk and he would have to leave his beautiful wife. One day Buddha went to their home and told him, "You must come along with me." Through his miraculous powers, the Buddha took Nanda to a jungle of monkeys without eyes. Buddha asked Nanda, "Who do you think is the prettiest, these monkeys or your wife?" Nanda answered, "There is no comparison, Puṇḍarīka is one hundred thousand times prettier than these monkeys." Then the Buddha with his miraculous powers took Nanda to a god realm filled with goddesses. He then asked him, "Which is more beautiful, these goddesses or Puṇḍarīka?" and Nanda answered, "Well, now that I look at these goddesses, Puṇḍarīka and the monkeys look pretty much the same." That is how interdependence makes some things look pretty and others look ugly. Objects are merely creations of the mind or mental concepts.

If one examines phenomena with logic and establishes that they are empty, one can gain an understanding of emptiness, but one doesn't gain a direct experience of emptiness. Also this logical method takes a long time. In the vajrayāna approach outer phenomena are understood to be empty; but the practice is to observe the mind. The mind is the source of all happiness and all suffering, the source of all craving and all anger, the source of all love and compassion; whatever occurs comes from the mind. When we first examine the mind, we think that it must be very powerful to create all this. However, looking inward, we are completely unable to find the mind; it is not outside the body, nor inside the body, nor in between these two. So the mind is empty. When we say the mind is empty, we don't mean that the mind doesn't exist like the "horns of a rabbit," which obviously do not exist. Nor is the emptiness of mind like empty space that has nothing in it. Rather the nature of mind is natural clarity. When we try to find the actual nature of mind directly, we cannot do so. It is both clarity and emptiness. When we examine mind, it is not just complete dullness or unconsciousness like a stone, but there is an uninterrupted continuum of clarity. The mind is normally full of thoughts and problems, but when we have understood the emptiness and clarity of the mind, then everything becomes very gentle and peaceful. So the text says the vipaśyanā in the vajrayāna has the nature of bliss.

The study of emptiness in the sūtras is the study of the *Prajñāpāramitā*. In the vajrayāna or tantra teachings the realization of emptiness is accomplished by looking at mind itself. Normally one thinks of the mind as being very strong and powerful, especially when all the thoughts and kleśas arise. But when one carefully examines to see where the mind actually is, one finds that there is nothing there, just a state of peace. This is called the state of great bliss because there is an absence of suffering and kleśas. While meditating one may think, "I cannot meditate because there are so many thoughts coming up." But when one examines where the thoughts come from and what they really are, one finds that they do not exist. There is just this natural state of peace. When I was very young, my teacher would tell me that all phenomena were empty, but I thought that this was impossible and could not be right. Later when studying the texts, I realized that phenomena were empty after all, but I did not see how the mind could be empty. There were so many thoughts and there was a power to all these thoughts and feelings, so it was impossible for the mind to be empty. But after receiving the instructions for meditation and analyzing the mind, I realized, "Oh, the mind is empty after all." So first one discovers that phenomena are empty, then one analyzes the mind and finds that it is also empty. With analysis it is easy to understand the emptiness of mind. What is difficult is to familiarize oneself with and habituate oneself to that understanding. Just to analyze the mind to see that its nature is empty is not very beneficial. For instance, when suffering begins it is of little help to simply think, "The nature of suffering is emptiness." But if one accustoms one's mind to the understanding of emptiness, then the mind poisons will be eliminated and suffering will be pacified.

So in this lifetime different kleśas such as anger have arisen and have been accepted as real. Sometimes anger becomes so strong that one falls under its power and says harsh things or even hits or kills someone. In the vajrayāna if anger arises, one thinks, "Previously I have fallen under its power, but this time I am going to look at the anger and determine what this anger is, where it came from, and where it is located now." When one examines the nature of anger in this way, one finds the anger is not there. One can't say, "This is the anger" or "This is what anger is like" or "The anger arises from this spot" or "The anger is created by this." It is like seeing someone in a film—there is an appearance of a person, but actually no one is there. In the same way, there is the appearance of anger, but it really isn't there. To realize this about anger, one doesn't analyze it logically, but one directly examines the nature of anger in oneself.

There are six root afflictions, or kleśas. The first is *anger,* so one looks for where anger first appears, where it comes from, where it stays, and so on. One does the same for the second kleśa, which is *craving* or *desire* for

external objects. The third kleśa is *ignorance* and the
fourth is *pride*. The fifth kleśa is *doubt* or *uncertainty*,
which has a positive or negative form. The sixth is
afflicted view, which means the belief in self, a clinging
to a self. These are the six root mind poisons as described in the commentaries. With each of these one
looks for where they first appear, where they dwell, and
where they go. This is analytic meditation and through
it one realizes the nature of the poisons. When one has
this realization, one rests one's mind in this realization.
In this way one obtains the realization of the emptiness
of things often described as the union of emptiness and
knowledge. This knowledge is clarity, an activity that
doesn't have any actual true nature because it is emptiness itself.[8] It is just a function, but not an actual thing
in itself. Clarity is like a quality or attribute, but there
is no basis to that quality. There is a process of knowing, but there is no knower who knows. Other than its
nature, it is just emptiness. So one has this union of
clarity and emptiness or this union of knowledge and
emptiness. Atīśa in his meditation instructions says that
normally we think of mind as being a combination of
past, present, and future thoughts. We put these together and think that it is mind. If we analyze it,
however, we find that past thoughts don't exist, that
they have gone and aren't there any more, that is, they
are nonexistent. Future thoughts have not yet been
created so they are naturally empty. So what we have is
just the present, which is a very brief period of time.
Examining the present mind is very difficult because we
find nothing there with any color, shape, form, or
nature. So we find present mind is not really anything
either and is therefore also empty.

Having understood the nature of emptiness through analytic meditation, we now look to see who is knowing, who has this understanding, and we find the knower doesn't exist. So we recognize this indivisibility of knowing and emptiness. This is known as discriminating wisdom or discriminating prajñā.

There are siddhas, that is, accomplished vajrayāna masters, who have said that when one looks directly at anger, the anger disappears. Anger has its own emptiness. It attains its own natural empty state. Previously, it has been said that there is no direct remedy that one can apply to anger that is correct in the context of hīnayāna and mahāyāna meditation. But in vajrayāna meditation there is the remedy of looking directly into the nature of anger.[9]

Categories of Vipaśyanā

There are three main categories of vipaśyanā: the vipaśyanās of the *four essences*, the vipaśyanā of the *three doorways*, and the vipaśyanā of the *six investigations*.

The four essences of vipaśyanā are described in the *Explanation of the View* sūtra and in Asaṅga's *Compendium of the Abhidharma*. In this analysis there are two categories of vipaśyanā—differentiation and complete differentiation. Each of these categories has two aspects—examination and analysis—so that there are actually four categories. Differentiation involves the understanding or prajñā that can distinguish between all the various kinds of phenomena. Complete differentiation is the understanding that distinguishes the actual nature of all phenomena. Examination is the gaining of an understanding of something on an obvious level.

84

Analysis is gaining an understanding on a very subtle level.

The vipaśyanās of the *four natures* are: (1) differentiation through examination, (2) differentiation through analysis, (3) complete differentiation through examination, and (4) complete differentiation through analysis. But in the *Explanation of the View* sūtra each of these four categories is divided again to make sixteen categories in all. The first category (differentiation through examination) is divided into four degrees of examination, namely (a) perfect examination, which means the examining is done very well, (b) definitive examination, in which a more complete understanding results, (c) perfect evaluation, which is even more complete, and (d) essential examination, which is the most complete. So each of these four essences of vipaśyanā has four degrees, making sixteen categories in all.

In the *Compendium of the Abhidharma* Asaṅga gives a description of the vipaśyanā with four essences in terms of their effect, that is, in terms of their activity. Asaṅga describes the first two essences of vipaśyanās, the differentiation of phenomena and the complete differentiation of phenomena, as remedies for negative propensities (Skt. *dausthulya,* Tib. *na ga len*) and the conceptualization of phenomena. The last two essences of vipaśyanā, through examination and through analysis, eliminate what needs to be eliminated, such as the mistaken beliefs about phenomena. With these eliminated one can rest in an unmistaken understanding.

In the *Explanation of the View* sūtra there is a description of the vipaśyanā of the *three doorways,* or entrances. In this sūtra Maitreya asks the Buddha, "How many kinds of vipaśyanā meditations are there?" The Buddha replies that there are three kinds. First, there is the vipaśyanā that arises from conceptual characteristics. If one meditates, for example, on selflessness one doesn't simply think about selflessness but one contemplates the reasons, proofs, and characteristics of selflessness. By going through these and thinking them over, one is able to develop a certain understanding of selflessness. One develops the insight that arises from contemplating the conceptual characteristics of something. The second of the vipaśyanās of the three doors is the insight that arises from investigation. Once one has developed the certainty of the first doorway, then one rests one's mind in that certainty and this is the second doorway. The third doorway arises from analysis. Because of familiarization with and habituation to certainty, one rests directly within the understanding of selflessness.

Next is the vipaśyanā of the *six investigations* into the characteristics of things. Three kinds of understanding come from these six investigations. First is *the investigation of meaning,* in which one has to investigate the words of the dharma and find out what is the meaning behind the words. Second is *the investigation of things* or the investigation of external phenomena and internal objects, which refers to mind and mental events. The understanding of the mind is arrived at through the understanding of the eight consciousnesses. The understanding of mental events is the understanding of the kleśas—the negativities of the mind. The investigation of external objects is the understanding of the external sensory experiences of sight, sound, smell, taste, and physical sensation. This is the understanding of the five aggregates of form, sensation, recognition, mental events, and consciousness, the twelve āyatanas, which are the source of perception and so on. Third is the *investigation of characteristics,* which is examining the object in more detail; for example, discovering that the visual consciousness perceives a visual object, the ear consciousness perceives sounds, etc. One examines the actual characteristics of all the different aspects in more detail. One investigates, for example, the visual form and identifies it as being the object of visual consciousness. Generally, there are two kinds of wisdom—the wisdom of the true nature of things and wisdom of the variety of things. First one has to examine all outer and inner objects to gain an understanding of their qualities. When one has attained this understanding, then one can understand their true nature.

The next three kinds of realization deal with the actual nature of things. These are the *investigation of direction, investigation of time,* and *investigation through reasoning.* We can easily understand emptiness with the investigation of direction and time. We normally think that there is a north, a south, an east, and a west. We think of directions as having an actual existence. We also talk about "here" and "there" as if there really were a "here" and a "there." But on closer examination, for example, one could say the wooden table in front of me is on the east side of the throne. When one moves the table a little, then one would say it is north of the throne. Direction, in fact, has no solid reality. So the investigation of direction leads to an understanding of emptiness.

The second investigation of the nature of things is the investigation of time. One usually thinks that there is a past, a present, and a future or one thinks in terms of a day, a month, a year, and so on. But when one examines this more closely, one finds that past does not really exist. Where is the present? One finds that other than being a conceptual projection on things, time has no reality of its own.

The third investigation of the nature of things is through reason. The Buddha said that his teachings should be examined and not taken on trust. For example, if one is buying gold, it wouldn't be correct to simply accept the seller's word that it is gold. One should test it by heating it with a flame to see whether it changes color. The gold might have a different metal inside so next one has to cut it open. Finally, there might be some fine particles of nongold in the lump. So one has to rub it against a stone to see if it is pure gold. In the same way, the Buddha said that his teachings should not be taken on trust, but one should engage in the process of investigation so that one can develop an understanding of the actual nature of things. Once one has gained this understanding, one can apply it to phenomena.

There are four kinds of reasoning. The first two relate to something arising from activity. The first is *the reasoning of dependence* and is involved with cause and effect. Using this reasoning, one can develop an understanding of how one's present life is due to events in a previous life. Since this is difficult to prove and understand, the Buddha taught cause and effect by reasoning, saying that if something exists, it is dependent and must have arisen from previous conditions or a cause. For example, a flower does not appear by itself but is dependent upon the previous conditions of a seed, soil, air, water, and so on. Many things have to come together for the flower to come into existence. So whatever exists is dependent upon previous causes and conditions. This is true of one's body and one's mind, which are the effect of previous causes and conditions in one's previous lifetimes.

The second kind of reasoning is *the reasoning of function*. This is the reasoning of dependent effect, which means that an effect depends on a particular cause. By understanding the first kind of reasoning and this second kind, one is able to avoid suffering by understanding that every cause has an effect and every effect has a causal condition. For example, in the Guru Rinpoche practice the mantra OM YE DHARMA HETU TRABOWA, etc., can be translated as "All phenomena arise from causes." The Buddha taught that all phenomena are an effect that had to arise due to a certain cause. The mantra says "All the causes have been explained by the Buddha." That is the second sentence in the mantra. If one wishes to attain perfect happiness, one must be able to find the correct cause of this happiness. To stop suffering, which is the result of causes, one must stop the causes of suffering. Therefore, one can find out how to eliminate suffering and attain happiness in the Buddha's teachings, which is done through the two kinds of reasoning—the reasoning of a cause having an effect and the reasoning of an effect being dependent on a cause. This means that whatever exists will create a result. Thus external objects or internal objects (such as the mind) will create results in the future. So the first reasoning of previous conditions proves previous lifetimes and the second reasoning of function proves future lifetimes.

The third kind of reasoning is the *reasoning of validity*, or how one knows something is true. There are three subtypes of this reasoning. First, one may experience something directly through seeing, hearing, or one of the other senses and this is called directly perceived validity. Second, there are things one cannot experience directly with the senses, but one understands them through logical deduction, or deduced validity. For example, the understanding of the emptiness of all phenomena or that a previous life must exist are examples of this second kind of knowledge. The third kind of reasoning is scriptural authenticity. One gains understanding by studying the teachings of the Buddha and of scholars and accomplished masters. There is a subject called *pramāṇa* in Sanskrit meaning "valid knowledge." There were two great masters of this in India—Dignāga and Dharmakīrti. Dignāga said there were three kinds of valid knowledge: that which is perceived directly; that which is obtained through deductive reasoning; and that which is received through scriptural authority. But then Dharmakīrti, the other great master of the pramāṇa, said that there are only two kinds of knowledge, direct knowledge and deductive analysis, because scriptural authority is understanding through examination and analysis, which is in fact the result of direct experience. So scriptural authority is encompassed by both of the other two kinds of knowledge and is not a separate third category.

The fourth kind of reasoning is the *reasoning of intrinsic nature*. There are two kinds of intrinsic reasons: relative intrinsic nature and absolute intrinsic nature. An example of the relative aspect is the fact that fire is hot and burns. One may ask, "What is the reason that fire is hot and burns?" But there really isn't any reason except that this is the intrinsic nature of fire. Similarly, one cannot ask, "Why is water wet?" because water is just wet and that is the intrinsic nature of water. Similarly, the nature of all phenomena is empty and that is just the intrinsic nature of all phenomena. There is no real reason why this is true, it is just something that has to be realized.

For example, in the beginning one isn't certain of the absence of a self or of the nature of emptiness. Through a process of reasoning, one can develop a definite understanding of selflessness and impermanence using logic. By going through these four reasonings, one develops certainty from analytical meditation and through this one gains clarity. Sometimes by doing this analytic meditation too much, one's mental stability decreases. If this happens, one does more nonanalytic meditation in which one just rests the mind without analyzing. This will bring about more stability.

There are six kinds of investigations—investigation of meaning, things, characteristics, directions, time, and reasoning—that can be used to gain an understanding of relative and absolute phenomena. Vipaśyanā can also be summed up into two types: preparatory vipaśyanā and actual vipaśyanā. Preparatory vipaśyanā, also known as discriminating vipaśyanā, is a preparation stage during which one investigates and analyzes in order to develop a definite understanding. In the actual stage, also called unwavering samādhi, one has gained definite understanding and the mind is able to dwell there.

The vipaśyanā of the four essences, six investigations, and three doorways are all analytical meditations. In general there are two kinds of meditation: the analytical meditation of the paṇḍita who is a scholar and the nonanalytical meditation or direct meditation of the *kusulu,* or simple yogi. So the analytical meditation of

the paṇḍita occurs when somebody examines and analyzes something thoroughly until a very clear understanding of it is developed. Doing this, one gains a very
definite and lasting understanding, so that there is no
danger of making an error. However, this path of the
paṇḍita takes a long time. The meditation of the kusulu
develops from knowing how to meditate, and then
meditating very extensively. This method is much
swifter, but there is a danger of going astray and making
a mistake. So one usually begins with an analysis and
examination of the reasons and proofs so that a definite
understanding is developed. Then one familiarizes oneself with this and develops an understanding and from
this one begins the kusulu meditation.

In analytical meditation, for example, one meditates
on selflessness, and in trying to identify the "self" one
finds that it doesn't exist internally, externally, or in
between. It is similar to śamatha meditation in that one
focuses the mind on an object, just as one rests the mind
on the in- and out-breath in śamatha meditation. Similarly, when resting on the absence of self, the mind is
kept focused one-pointedly on this and just rests, and
from this develops the experience of the certainty of the
absence of self. It is the same method employed in
śamatha meditation so it is called the analytical meditation on the absence of self.

Analytic meditation is not just hearing, receiving,
and contemplating the teachings. Instead it is the definite insight one has gained united with śamatha meditation. In śamatha meditation one focuses the mind on
breathing or focuses it on no object whatsoever. Here
one has definite knowledge that is gained through analytic deduction. This knowledge is joined together with

the stability of mind in śamatha and one meditates on the union of these two. This is what is meant by analytic meditation.

The direct, nonanalytical meditation is called kusulu meditation in Sanskrit. This was translated as *trömeh* in Tibetan, which means "without complication" or being very simple without the analysis and learning of a great scholar. Instead, the mind is relaxed and without applying analysis so it just rests in its nature. In the sūtra tradition, there are some nonanalytic meditations, but mostly this tradition uses analytic meditation.

Methods of Vipaśyanā

The basis of vipaśyanā meditation is a state of samādhi, a meditation state without thoughts and concepts. Its primary quality is that it cuts through all the misconceptions, inaccuracies, and misunderstandings we might have. It says in the text that it is necessary to have the viewpoint of the absence of self and without this viewpoint we cannot develop genuine vipaśyanā meditation. Therefore, we have to develop this understanding of the absence of self. The text states that if we don't have an understanding of what the meditation should be directed at, we are like a person without arms trying to hold onto the side of a cliff. So the basis of meditation is the definite understanding of the absence of self. We need to first recognize this, then contemplate it until we have a definite understanding of the absence of self. Once we have developed this understanding, then the mind must be able to rest upon this understanding— relaxed and completely unagitated. If we have the view, but just think intellectually about it, we will not be able to properly develop our meditation because we won't be able to eliminate the obscurations. Hence the text says that even if we are learned and have studied and understood the view of the absence of self, but have not meditated on it, we are like a miser with great wealth who can't use any of it because of his stinginess. Not only is all of the wealth of a miser of no use to him, but it is also of no good to others because he doesn't give it to anyone. Similarly if we have the understanding and view of the absence of self, without meditation we won't derive any benefit from it because we are not able to develop wisdom and eliminate the kleśas. We also then cannot benefit others because we are not able to follow the path and gain enlightenment.

To summarize, to develop the view of the absence of self, one has to meditate. One needs to study first the teachings of selflessness, then analyze and contemplate them so that one can develop a definite understanding of this view. Then one rests one's mind on that, focused in that view but in a completely relaxed state. This resting is like the union of stability of mind and insight, the union of śamatha and vipaśyanā. One must balance the analytic meditation that develops clarity of mind with stability of mind. Too much analytic meditation will reduce one's stability. Therefore, one must relax the mind in a nonanalytic state of meditation. Too much nonanalytic meditation will diminish the clarity of mind and one begins to sink into dullness. So one then does repeated analytic meditation to regain one's balance. Developing both clarity and stability will make the mind very powerful. Generally, the main practice of all the schools in Tibet was first to analyze phenomena repeatedly to gain an understanding of the view and having done this, to then rest the mind in nonanalytic meditation.

Emptiness is the essence of the dharma teachings because it is the way we eliminate all the mind poisons and faults. So selflessness and emptiness are very important. Emptiness can become an obstacle to our understanding of karma and our practice of good actions because we may think, "Everything is emptiness, nothing exists, so I don't have to practice dharma." So there is danger involved in this teaching on emptiness. Nāgārjuna said that we have to understand emptiness correctly, otherwise it will have a bad effect. In India siddhas would pick up poisonous snakes. Through the power of their mantras on the snake they would be able to perform miracles and increase prosperity by holding the snake. Without the power of meditation and the power of the mantra anyone holding a poisonous snake would be bitten. In the same way, if we have a good understanding of emptiness, it helps to develop our meditation, but if we have a mistaken idea of emptiness and think there is no need to do good actions, we are in danger of developing an obstacle to our dharma practice.

One has the accumulation of merit and the accumulation of wisdom in dharma practice. The accumulation of wisdom is śamatha and the accumulation of merit is vipaśyanā meditation. The accumulation of merit is done with a pure motivation. One has a very special object for one's actions and for that object one develops faith and makes prayers of supplications and offerings. Sometimes one's meditation will become very clear and it will develop. Sometimes one's meditation will not go well and it will not make progress. At that time one must develop wisdom to accumulate merit. So one develops faith and devotion and makes offerings, prayers of supplication to the sublime or sacred objects, and also practices whatever good actions one can to accumulate merit, a state of good karma. Through that one will increase the accumulation of wisdom.

There is another approach that is the tradition of Ganden monastery—a Gelug tradition. In this tradition even when resting in meditation, one thinks of the knowledge one has acquired on egolessness and one maintains this knowledge by repeatedly thinking "This is like this" and "That is like that," and so on, bringing up the teaching again and again.

As mentioned before, when one has developed śamatha meditation, many different kinds of thoughts and images from internal and external events appear in the mind. These are called unexamined images. This means that they are not actual external images, but are just the appearance of things, images that arise in the mind. In vipaśyanā meditation one takes these images and analyzes them to develop the conviction that they have no true existence of their own. In this method the mind is turned inward. For example, one doesn't look at a pillar and think, "Well, this is a pillar and the pillar has no reality of its own," and so on. Instead one examines whatever appears in the mind and sees that it has no existence of its own. What one needs in this meditation is discriminating knowledge so that all things are seen as distinct from each other. One needs discriminating knowledge in meditation because one needs to be able to focus on particular objects in meditation. Nothing becomes mixed or overlapping so things do not turn out to be vague, indistinct, or unclear.

There are good mental events and bad mental events. There are also events that are continuously present in the mind and events that are transitory. In fact, there are fifty-one different mental events, of which samādhi and prajñā are just two (see table 3, pages 98–100). This means that everyone has samādhi and prajñā, but what differs between individuals is the strength of these two events. One must increase the power of one's samādhi so that one's mind becomes more stable. The mental event of prajñā is also present in all persons, but it must be developed and increased with samādhi so that one can develop a clear and definite understanding. One needs to have both of these to develop vipaśyanā, with samādhi giving the stability and prajñā giving the ability to analyze the details of everything and develop a thorough understanding of them.

In the *Compendium of the Abhidharma* Asaṅga says that vipaśyanā possesses samādhi and prajñā. There are two general kinds of phenomena: that which is perceived (a percept such as a sound) and that which perceives. The sixth consciousness contains things that are perceived. So what is perceived in the mind is also classified as a percept. There are six kinds of percepts (sight, sound, smell, taste, body sensations, and objects of the sixth consciousness). Internally one has consciousness, which is the perceiver. For example, a visual object is perceived by the sense organ and there is the perceiver, which is visual consciousness. There are five sensory consciousnesses and a mental consciousness that identifies what is good or bad, remembers, and so on. Sometimes the mind focuses on external percepts and when they appear not to possess any reality, this is known as the external indivisibility of appearance and emptiness. "Empty"

The Fifty-one Mental Factors (Chaitasika)

THE FIVE OMNIPRESENT MENTAL FACTORS
(Sarvatraga)

Feeling	*(vedanā)*
Discernment	*(saṃjñā)*
Intention	*(chetanā)*
Contact	*(sparśa)*
Mental engagement	*(manasikāra)*

THE FIVE DETERMINING MENTAL FACTORS
(Viṣayaniyata)

Aspiration	*(chhanda)*
Belief	*(adhimoskṣa)*
Recollection	*(smṛiti)*
Stabilization	*(samādhi)*
Superior knowledge	*(prajñā)*

THE ELEVEN VIRTUOUS MENTAL FACTORS
(Kuśala)

Faith	*(śraddhā)*
Shame	*(hrī)*
Embarrassment	*(apatrāpya)*
Detachment	*(alobha)*
Nonhatred	*(adveṣa)*
Nonbewilderment	*(amoha)*
Joyous effort	*(vīrya)*

Suppleness	(*praśrabdhi*)
Conscientiousness	(*apramāda*)
Equanimity	(*upekṣā*)
Nonharmfulness	(*avihiṃsā*)

THE SIX ROOT MENTAL DEFILEMENTS
(*Mūlakleśa*)

Desire	(*rāga*)
Anger	(*pratigha*)
Pride	(*māna*)
Ignorance	(*avidyā*)
Doubt	(*vichikitsā*)
Afflicted view	(*dṛiṣṭi*)

THE TWENTY SECONDARY DEFILEMENTS
(*Upakleśa*)

Wrath	(*krodha*)
Resentment	(*upanāha*)
Concealment	(*mrakṣa*)
Spite	(*pradāsa*)
Jealousy	(*īrṣyā*)
Avarice	(*mātsarya*)
Deceit	(*māyā*)
Dishonesty	(*śāṭhya*)
Self-importance	(*mada*)
Harmfulness	(*vihiṃsā*)
Nonshame	(*āhrīkya*)
Nonembarrassment	(*anapatrāpya*)

99

Lethargy	(*styāna*)
Agitation	(*auddhatya*)
Nonfaith	(*āśraddhya*)
Laziness	(*kausīdya*)
Nonconscientiousness	(*pramāda*)
Forgetfulness	(*muṣitasmṛititā*)
Distraction	(*vikṣepa*)
Nonintrospection	(*asaṃprajanya*)

THE FOUR CHANGEABLE MENTAL FACTORS
(*Aniyata*)

Contrition	(*kaukṛitya*)
Sleep	(*middha*)
Examination	(*vitarka*)
Analysis	(*vichāra*)

here does not mean that there is no appearance, but that the nature of that appearance is emptiness. For example, when one is dreaming of an elephant, the nature of that elephant is emptiness because there is no reality to it. If someone asked whether you were dreaming of an elephant, you would say yes, and this demonstrates that the appearance of the elephant was there. But the actual nature of the elephant is still emptiness.

An example of meditating on the internal perceiver is anger. Anger arises and one examines it not with ordinary understanding, but with discriminating knowledge. One asks where does it come from or what is its source? This is not in terms of "this person did this to me and that made me angry," but in terms of where did the anger arise from. One looks for its origination and where it is now. Is it inside the body or outside the body or between these two? One analyzes with discriminating prajñā and tries to discover its location and its nature—what is it like, what color, what shape? With awareness one finds that there is a clarity in the anger and at the same time it is empty of reality. With discriminating knowledge one discovers that it is the union of emptiness and awareness.[10]

This same way of meditating is also used for the six principal mind poisons (kleśas). The first mind poison is *anger* and second is *attachment* to things such as food, wealth, one's body, and so on. When attachment is examined in the same way that anger was examined, one is unable to find any reality to the attachment and discovers that it is the union of emptiness and awareness. The third mind poison is *pride* or seeing oneself as superior to others. On closer examination, however, it is also the union of emptiness and awareness. The fourth mind poison is *ignorance,* and this is different from the others because it does not arise so vividly and is more pervasive. There are two kinds of ignorance: mixed ignorance and isolated ignorance. If ignorance accompanies one of the other mind poisons such as anger, so that one is not aware of the nature of the anger or does not realize that one is going to make a mistake because of anger, this is mixed ignorance. Isolated ignorance is not understanding the nature of phenomena. On closer examination one finds that ignorance also has no solid reality and is the union of emptiness and awareness. The fifth mind poison is *uncertainty*, which means that whatever one's mind is focused on, one can't make a decision. There are two kinds of uncertainty: favorable

uncertainty and unfavorable uncertainty. Favorable uncertainty occurs when one thinks something probably
is and unfavorable uncertainty is when one thinks something probably isn't. So in a decision a person with
favorable uncertainty will think yes and a person with
unfavorable uncertainty will think no. On closer examination this mind poison also is the inseparability of
emptiness and awareness. The sixth mind poison is
called the *nature of the view* and is the mistaken view that
"I exist." So there is a misconception in what one
believes and when one examines it closely with discriminating understanding, one finds it also doesn't have any
reality and is the indivisibility of emptiness and
awareness.

In vipaśyanā meditation one meditates on the mind
poisons as being the inseparability of emptiness and
awareness. One can also meditate on neutral thoughts.
Neutral thoughts are thoughts that are neither good nor
bad. There are two kinds of neutral thoughts: creative
neutral thoughts and thoughts of activity. Creative neutral thoughts are something like "I want to make din-
ner" and neutral thoughts of activity are something like
"I must leave" or "I want to go to eat." These thoughts
are neutral but one can examine them to see who is
thinking the thought "I want to eat" and where this
thought is located. One discovers that the nature of
neutral thoughts is that they have no reality and are the
indivisibility of emptiness and awareness.

One therefore examines the internal understanding of
the indivisibility of emptiness and awareness and the
external understanding of the indivisibility of emptiness
and appearance. The discriminating knowledge understands this indivisibility, and one realizes that the dis-

criminating knowledge also has no reality, so that the mind rests in the percept, the perceiver, and the understanding of these two. For example, in the past one rubbed two sticks together to make a fire and when the fire was started, it burned up the two sticks as well. In the same way, the understanding of the indivisibility of emptiness and awareness, and of emptiness and appearance, also has the nature of emptiness. The practice instructions of Atīśa say the mind of the past has ceased to exist and the mind of the future has not come into existence. The present mind is difficult to examine because it has no color, shape, or location. It is just like space—it is unborn and it is not one or many things. Even though it is empty, the clarity of mind never ceases. There is this continuous clarity of mind and the mind never becomes blank or like a stone. One also can't locate where this clarity comes from.

The meditational state of vipaśyanā is described as having no appearances, which means that there is the realization of the inseparability of emptiness and appearances do not have any reality of their own. In spite of this emptiness, there is the unceasing clarity of mind that has no reality of its own so the mind in meditation is free from any complications or elaborations. It is not "existent" and it is not "nonexistent" and it is not "neither existent nor nonexistent" and it is not "both existent and nonexistent." It is free from these four complications and is neither created or something that ceases. Because if it existed, then it must be born and if it is born then it must also die (cease to exist). But there is nothing there to be born or die. Through this realization one can eliminate the defects of dullness and agitation in meditation. With these removed, there is no clinging or grasping, the mind doesn't think "This is good and has to be kept" and "This is bad and has to be rejected." This is what is meant by vipaśyanā meditation.

The Accomplishment of Vipaśyanā

Gampopa said that to obtain the definitive view, one needs to look at the nature of the mind. There is no sense in looking elsewhere. A Tibetan story describes this. There was a man named Je, which means "strongman." He was very strong but stupid and had a jewel embedded in his forehead. When he became tired, the skin of his forehead sagged down and completely covered the jewel in his forehead. When he put his hand up to feel the jewel, he could not feel it because the skin was completely covering it and so he thought that he had lost the jewel. He then went looking for the jewel, but couldn't find it anywhere. In the same way, it is said that to obtain a definitive view, one has to look in the mind itself and there is no point looking for it elsewhere.

When one has the realization of the mind, it is said there is no appearance, which means that when one looks at the mind one can't find that it exists as an actual thing. There is also the aspect of clarity, which is the awareness of the absence of any true existence. This is an awareness that never ceases or is lost. Then there is the absence of all elaborations or fabrications, which means there is no complication in one's life because one has realized that there is no actual thing. So one can say there isn't a complication of nonexistence because there is the aspect of clarity. One can't say that it is completely void, a vacuum, because there is the clarity of this awareness. Therefore, it has no existence nor is it non-existent, so it has no actual nature.

The third Karmapa, Ranjung Dorje, in his *Mahāmudrā Prayer* says that the mind does not exist because it cannot be seen by the buddhas. So the mind has no true existence as a thing because we cannot find it. Not only can't we find the mind, but the buddhas can't either. We may think that if the mind does not exist as a thing, then it must be nonexistent. But the second line of this verse says that mind is not nonexistent because it is the basis of saṃsāra and nirvāṇa. So it is not nonexistent because of all the appearances of saṃsāra and the way saṃsāra arises in the mind. Therefore it can't be nonexistent. Also the attainment of nirvāṇa, Buddhahood, the knowledge of the true nature and of the variety of phenomena develop from the mind. Therefore it is not nonexistent. The third line says there is no contradiction in saying that it is neither existent nor nonexistent. In fact this is not a contradiction. This is the Middle Way, which is free from the extremes of existence and non-existence. So the meaning in this *Mahāmudrā Prayer* by the Karmapa is the same as has been given here. It says that this awareness is completely without the mindfulness of thinking "There is this," "There is that," "This is good," "This is bad," and so on. There isn't any kind of mental activity or mental attention in thinking. This is eliminated and the awareness is in a completely relaxed state. We rest in meditation in this way and this is how Atīśa describes the meditation and the way we should practice.

Previously, being "well trained" was described as a characteristic of the accomplishment of śamatha. The

THE PRACTICE OF TRANQUILLITY & INSIGHT

accomplishment of vipaśyanā is also the state of being "completely trained." One may be able to meditate but later not do so well because one loses one's clarity, or one's mind becomes dull, or one loses one's wish to meditate. But when one has reached the state of the suppleness of being well trained, then the mind naturally engages in vipaśyanā and this vipaśyanā brings clarity and understanding. So until one has accomplished the suppleness of being well trained, one has not attained true vipaśyanā. The text says that the nature of this vipaśyanā and the way it is created has already been explained in the śamatha section. In terms of the abhidharma one can say being "well trained" is a mental event and therefore all beings possess it all the time. But what differs between beings is its extent. Some beings naturally engage in negative actions and some naturally engage in good actions. But since we haven't been meditating from beginningless time, we are not "well trained" in our meditation. We don't have this natural tendency, so we have to habituate ourselves to it as we did for śamatha practice. The "well-trained" vipaśyanā will gradually develop by beginning with very little and then gradually increase. Samādhi, understanding, mindfulness, and awareness are all mental events that are naturally present, but must be increased. So first we develop śamatha meditation and then we develop vipaśyanā. The development of the "well-trained" vipaśyanā is described in the *Explanation of the View* sūtra, which says that there are two kinds of realization. There is the realization of the entire multiplicity of phenomena, which is understanding the relative aspect of phenomena. This is the understanding of impermanence, the five aggregates, and the twelve links of dependent origination. To develop this we have to have a perfectly trained mind. Second, there is the realization of the true nature of phenomena and to have this, one also needs a perfectly trained mind. If one doesn't have a completely trained mind, then one will not have these two realizations or genuine vipaśyanā. So the development of the completely trained mind is the sign of the accomplishment of vipaśyanā.

To summarize, there is the state of being "well trained" in which one is able to do vipaśyanā meditation without any difficulty or hardship; it is very pleasant and easy to do. So when doing vipaśyanā meditation, there is no mental or physical difficulty. This is the sign of the accomplishment of vipaśyanā meditation.

PART THREE

UNION
[*zung 'jug*]

5

THE UNION OF ŚAMATHA
AND VIPAŚYANĀ

ONE can't achieve enlightenment with just śamatha meditation. One also can't achieve enlightenment with just vipaśyanā meditation.
No one achieves wisdom of Buddhahood with just
vipaśyanā meditation. What is necessary is to study
śamatha by itself, then study vipaśyanā by itself, and
then practice the union of śamatha and vipaśyanā to
reach final enlightenment. The original text divides this
chapter into three parts: the practice of the union of
śamatha and vipaśyanā, the timing of this union, and
the different kinds of śamatha and vipaśyanā.

The Practice of This Union

The union of the stability of mind (*śamatha*) and of
insight (*vipaśyanā*) occurs when the mind is at rest and
still, not in the ordinary way, but at rest in the wisdom
of the *dharmadhātu*. In the sūtra tradition there are four
different sets of instructions on how to do this, each of
which is given by a different Indian master. The instructions vary, but they agree that one should practice the
union of śamatha and vipaśyanā. These four masters are
Bhāvaviveka, Śāntideva, Kamalaśīla, and Chandrakīrti,
who were all Madhyamaka masters concerned with a

III

thorough understanding of emptiness. There are two major schools in the Madhyamaka: the Svātantrikas and the Prāsaṅgikas. To simplify, the Svātantrika school says that on the level of ultimate truth nothing has any true existence, whereas on the relative level things exist. So the Svātantrika school is concerned with concepts of existence and nonexistence. The Prāsaṅgika school, however, believes that things have no actual nature and phenomena are just appearances, that apart from these appearances they don't have any true nature. All things are just appearances. So the Prāsaṅgikas are not so concerned with concepts of existence and nonexistence.

First, Bhāvaviveka of the Prāsaṅgika school uses the method for developing union of śamatha and vipaśyanā, which is that one first meditates on unpleasantness and love, etc. This is described in the section on the remedy for attachment where, for example, one meditates on love to overcome clinging to anger. A person thus develops śamatha meditation. Then one analyzes phenomena. In the analysis of external phenomena one develops an understanding of the inseparability of appearance and emptiness. In the analysis of internal phenomena one gains understanding of the inseparability of emptiness and awareness of the perceiver.

Second, Śāntideva in *A Guide to the Bodhisattva's Way of Life* says that to develop śamatha one needs to develop *bodhichitta*. There is relative and absolute bodhichitta and in this practice one develops śamatha through relative bodhichitta by wishing that all beings achieve happiness and be free from suffering. But beings do not know what causes suffering and so they remain in suffering. Therefore, one must develop the motivation to help all beings become free from suffering. However, since one doesn't have this ability, one practices dharma because the dharma will teach one how to do this. One thinks that one is going to accomplish the goal of helping all beings attain the state of Buddhahood. This is the development of relative bodhichitta with śamatha. After achieving the completely trained state of this śamatha, one moves on to vipaśyanā. Through the development of vipaśyanā comes the realization of emptiness. This is the same as Bhāvaviveka's analysis of outer phenomena and inner phenomena to develop the understanding of the inseparability of emptiness and appearance; and the inseparability of emptiness and awareness respectively.

The third system, that of Kamalaśīla, is widely practiced and can be found in the second volume of the *Stages of Meditation*. One develops śamatha through resting the mind on an external object such as a statue of the Buddha, then on an internal object such as the breath and so on. This practice makes the mind still and calm. Having developed śamatha this way, one then develops vipaśyanā by analyzing and examining that mind resting in śamatha. One begins to realize that there is no mind that can be identified and develops an understanding of the inseparability of awareness and emptiness. One recognizes that when the mind is examined, there is nothing there that can be identified. One develops vipaśyanā meditation through the analysis of the six root mind poisons, as has been described in the tradition of Atīśa in the śamatha section.

Chandrakīrti, a very great Madhyamaka master, composed the text *Entering the Middle Way,* which presents many kinds of reasoning and logical analyses of emptiness. Not only did he give reasons, but to eliminate his pupils' clinging to phenomena he did a practical demonstration. At the entrance of most temples there is a painting of the Wheel of Existence.[11] In the past arhats would go and visit the six realms, and when they returned, they would describe to others what it was like so that ordinary people could listen to these teachings and have these realms described to them. So the Buddha said that at the entrance to the temples there should be a painting of the beings of the six realms for ordinary people to see. Anyway, in the painting of the six realms there are depicted some cows in the section of the animal realm. One day Chandrakīrti came up to the painting and began milking one of the cows in the painting. He was able to get enough milk for everyone to drink. He did this to demonstrate that whether it was a painting of a cow or an actual cow, neither has any true reality. So Chandrakīrti was not only a great scholar, but also had great realization.

Chandrakīrti's method is different from the others. In this method one listens to the teachings and then contemplates them so that one gains understanding of the true nature of things. By listening to and contemplating the teachings, one develops the prajñā or understanding of the true nature of all phenomena, which develops the view that comes from the analysis of the suchness of things. One first develops this perfect understanding of the true nature of phenomena, and having gained this, one develops śamatha and vipaśyanā meditation. Thus they are practiced on the basis of the view, the actual understanding of the nature of mind.

In these four systems there are slightly different instructions on how to develop śamatha and vipaśyanā, but these are slight variations. They agree that we first need to stabilize the mind, then we will be able to develop the insight of vipaśyanā and that these two practices are not separate, but are a union. They agree that the practice of śamatha is a causal condition resulting in vipaśyanā, and that we practice the union of these two together. This means the mind must be one-pointed and not distracted by other thoughts. This also means that we use the mind as the object of our meditation and do not think about something else. This one-pointedness comes when we are resting in meditation, not while we are analyzing phenomena.

There is a lama named Mendong Lama Sherab who is from Lachi, a place where Milarepa meditated. This is a very isolated place near the border of Nepal and Tibet. When the Chinese invaded, the border was closed and there was no passage through there, and so it became a very isolated place to which no one ever came. There was a cave there in which Lama Sherab meditated for three years. When I was talking with Lama Sherab about his experiences, I said, "You must have had a lot of realizations and experiences there because there was nothing there to distract you." Lama Sherab replied, "If you sit alone in a cave, your mind still becomes distracted." If you don't control your mind, your mind will become distracted. It is important when meditating to have control over the mind so that it won't become distracted. Therefore, the meditation has to be under firm control to protect it from arising thoughts.

The text describes all the various kinds of śamatha and vipaśyanā because it is a *"Treasury" of Knowledge* presenting all knowledge. The above practices are those that are taught in the sūtra tradition. What is practiced in the vajrayāna tradition is the system of Kamalaśīla using an external, then internal object, etc. So śamatha is generally developed by doing the practice of watching one's breath.

Vipaśyanā is normally practiced using the different analyses of external objects and emptiness, internal emptiness and awareness, using the many different methods that have been described. But the way followed in the vajrayāna tradition is the internal inseparability of emptiness and awareness. When meditation is stable, the mind rests in its natural stability. Sometimes thoughts arise and the mind is then in movement. One looks to see what is the nature of the movement of the mind. This is not using analytical reasoning and logic, but having a direct experience of the nature of mind at rest and in movement. This is the usual method followed for the development of vipaśyanā.

One doesn't have to logically analyze the mind to find out that it has no existence. One can just look at the mind and see that it is not there. At the same time there is this process of knowing or awareness. The word for "mind" in Tibetan is *sem* or *shepa,* which means "that which knows."[12] So there is this knowing, but if one tries to find out what it is that is knowing, one can't find anything. The activity of knowing is unceasing but one can't find anything that knows so one can say that this is selflessness. When there is no mind, there is selflessness and there is emptiness so one can call this the inseparability of clarity and emptiness. This selflessness, or egolessness, is something that we haven't really thought of throughout beginningless time that we have been in saṃsāra because our attention has been turned outward. But turning inward, one sees this selflessness and the inseparability of clarity and emptiness. This emptiness, however, is not emptiness meaning nothing whatsoever because there is the interdependence of phenomena, the awareness of what we experience, the forms we see, the sounds we hear, and so on.

If our mind is not under control, then all the obscurations can arise in the mind. So all these things appear and their experience is something like watching a movie. There is nothing actually there in the theater, yet all these pictures, sounds, and emotions appear in our mind. So we have appearances arising in mind, but when we investigate more closely, we see that it has no true existence, but is just the interdependence of phenomena (such as the movie projector, the film, the screen, the speakers, etc.).

The third Karmapa, Rangjung Dorje, described the nature of śamatha and vipaśyanā in the vajrayāna tradition. In śamatha there are obvious and subtle waves of thoughts that become naturally pacified. He said that these obvious and subtle thoughts become stilled; they are like the sea. There are sometimes large and sometimes small waves on the sea. When these waves cease, then the sea is completely still without movement. In the same way, one has sometimes subtle and sometimes obvious thoughts. If these become completely pacified, the mind becomes totally still, calm, and unmoving like a calm sea. Even when the sea is completely still, there can be some pollution, so one needs to have very pure and clear water running into the sea for it to be completely pure. Likewise, even though the mind has been stilled, there can still be the defect of dullness of the mind. So correct śamatha occurs when the defect of dullness is removed so that there is a state of calm and stability and also a state of clarity.

Rangjung Dorje also describes vipaśyanā as looking again and again at something that cannot be seen. So the nature of mind cannot be examined or analyzed. He says that one looks at the nature of mind again and again and nothing with true existence can be found. By looking at this and seeing the true nature of the mind, one becomes free of doubt and uncertainty of what the mind is like. Instead one develops a certainty through seeing the nature of the mind, and this is vipaśyanā meditation.

To develop śamatha and vipaśyanā you have to have diligence and apply yourself to meditation without going from one method to another. But diligence alone is not enough without having the actual practice and essential instructions such as in guru yoga. In this practice you supplicate the guru and in this way you develop devotion to the guru. Following this supplication and development of faith and devotion to the guru, light beams of white, red, and blue come from the guru (who is visualized in front of you) and merge into yourself; thus you receive the blessing from the guru. When that occurs, a transformation in meditation can occur. If you hadn't been able to develop the insight of vipaśyanā meditation, then suddenly through guru yoga you can develop this meditation. If you have had the experience of śamatha and vipaśyanā, guru yoga can help increase the intensity of this experience. The purifications of your bad karma and the accumulation of merit will also increase your śamatha and vipaśyanā. The elimination of your bad karma and obscurations will also remove obstacles to your śamatha and vipaśyanā. Therefore, you do the practice of Vajrasattva for the purification of your bad karma and obscurations and do the practice of

maṇḍala offering to help your experience and realization. The four preliminary practices are very important
and the purpose of doing these practices is to increase
your śamatha and vipaśyanā. You need diligence to
practice meditation, but diligence by itself is not
enough, so you get help from the practice of the preliminaries. The first preliminary, prostrations, is taking
refuge in the three jewels (of Buddha, dharma, and
saṅgha) and the development of bodhichitta, which
causes you to enter on the genuine path, and the other
three preliminaries increase the development of śamatha
and vipaśyanā. The primary cause for the development
of śamatha and vipaśyanā is your own diligence and the
necessary conditions are the preliminary practices. Having both of these enables you to develop the union of
śamatha and vipaśyanā.

The Time of the Union

The text says that there are two kinds of union: śamatha
and vipaśyanā with a reference point and śamatha and
vipaśyanā without a reference point. Śamatha with a
reference point means that one's mind is focused on
something like a statue of the Buddha or the breath.
Vipaśyanā with a reference point means that one analyt-
ically examines and differentiates between phenomena.
When that vipaśyanā's realization arises together with
nonconceptual śamatha, there is the union of the two.
Though there is śamatha and vipaśyanā that depends on
a reference point, the main kind of śamatha and vipaśyanā is nonconceptual śamatha and vipaśyanā that is
without a reference point. This kind of śamatha meditation is described by Ranjung Dorje when he talks of

the large and subtle waves becoming stilled. This is the state where one rests in the nature of the mind without any concepts. It is the state of stability. The vipaśyanā is seeing that the mind does not have any reality or true existence. The presence of this state of peace and the realization of the nature of the mind is the union of śamatha and vipaśyanā. Śamatha is an aid to the vipaśyanā and the vipaśyanā is an aid to the śamatha. So it is called the union of śamatha and vipaśyanā.

Nonconceptual śamatha meditation is the mind just resting in its natural state. Nonconceptual vipaśyanā is understanding the inseparability of the appearances and emptiness of external phenomena and understanding the inseparability of the awareness and emptiness of the internal perceiver. Both are necessary in order to have the nonconceptual śamatha and vipaśyanā united as a single identity. So one can practice śamatha alone or one can practice vipaśyanā alone but when they are practiced together they should be practiced in union. The union means that śamatha and vipaśyanā are not coexisting with each other, but instead it is impossible to differentiate between them. So if there's nonconceptual śamatha, then there will be nonconceptual vipaśyanā, or if there is nonconceptual vipaśyanā, then there will be nonconceptual śamatha.

The union of śamatha and vipaśyanā is explained clearly by Kamalaśīla in the first volume of the *Stages of Meditation*. He says that when practicing meditation one sees the absence of the essence of phenomena. Being a Mādhyamaka explanation, the statement means that one sees the emptiness of phenomena, which means seeing the true nature of phenomena exactly as it is. This is described by the Buddha as being beyond words and thoughts. Beyond words means that the state completely transcends the ability to be described by words. Being beyond thoughts means one cannot analyze it conceptually by thinking that it exists, or doesn't exist, or whatever. One also cannot say that phenomena are nonexistent because there is the awareness of mind. This direct insight into the clarity and the absence of any true essence is vipaśyanā—true insight.

What then is the śamatha aspect? This is the absence of dullness or agitation in meditation. There is also the absence of the three obstacles of aggression and doubt and regret, which can hinder the development of a stable meditative state. If one has regret, one thinks, "Oh, I wish such and such a thing had happened" or "This thing didn't turn out right," which disrupts meditation. If one has doubt, one thinks, "Is this true or isn't it?" and this uncertainty disrupts meditation. If one has aggression, one feels anger toward someone and this will disrupt meditation. So in meditation one is free from dullness and agitation and the three obstacles of regret, doubt, and aggression; so there is no deliberate activity. "No deliberate activity" means that one rests in the natural state of concentration due to familiarization. With this familiarization one doesn't need to make a deliberate effort to stay in meditation. The text says that when one is able to see the actual nature of meditation and phenomena and be free from the defects of agitation and dullness, etc., and when one can rest effortlessly in meditation free from any deliberate action, then one has achieved the union of śamatha and vipaśyanā.

The way of practicing the union of śamatha and vipaśyanā meditation was described by Milarepa in his songs, particularly the song to Nyima Paldar Bum. Paldar Bum had a lot of faith and was very skilled in her dharma practice. She was also very good at asking sharp and intelligent questions. Milarepa met her one time when he was giving teachings to a number of people. She felt great faith in Milarepa and invited him into her home. She told him that she was living in saṃsāra and during the day she was busy preparing food and clothing and in the evening she slept. But she wanted to practice the dharma and asked Milarepa what practice she could do that would lead her to attain Buddhahood.

Milarepa then sang her a spiritual song (dohā) in which he used a number of metaphors and examples. When I was young my teacher told me the story of Milarepa leaving his homeland, having his house destroyed, and later returning to his home to see the ruins. I heard the song in which Milarepa described his ruined house as a lion's upper jaw and a neighboring house as being like a donkey's ears. When I heard this song as a child, I thought it was some kind of metaphor. Later when I returned to Tibet and saw all the ruined buildings, I thought, "This really does look like a lion's jaw and that's like a donkey's ears with bits of the buildings fallen down and pieces sticking up." Milarepa's metaphor perfectly described what the ruins looked like.

Returning to our story, Milarepa gave Paldar Bum a teaching in a song in which he used four metaphors or symbols. He first said to her, "Look at the sky. The sky has no center that you can point to and you can't determine where the edge of the sky is. In that same way rest in your mind without there being a center or limit." Second, he said, "Look at the mountain. It is completely stable and unmoving. In that way your mind should be firm and steady." Third, he said, "Look at the sun and moon. They don't fluctuate in brightness. They stay completely clear with the same intensity all the time. In that way your mind's clarity should not fluctuate." And fourth, he said, "Look at a great lake that has no waves and is completely calm and still. In that way your mind should be calm and still." Milarepa did not mean that we should actually meditate on a mountain, sun, lake, or the sky, but these were metaphors for nonconceptual meditation we should have. Then Milarepa told Paldar Bum to meditate without concepts, which is the śamatha aspect. Looking at the essence of the absence of thoughts is the vipaśyanā aspect. So he instructed her to meditate with the union of śamatha and vipaśyanā by telling her to meditate without thoughts. To meditate without thoughts is the fifth instruction in this song.

Nyima Paldar Bum meditated and came back to Milarepa with questions about the song given her. She said that when she looked at the sky, she was able to meditate like the sky in a completely relaxed state. But clouds appeared in the sky, and what should she do about the clouds? She said that she was able to meditate on the mountains. But when doing this, she could see plants and trees growing on the mountains, and what should she do about them? She said that she was able to meditate like the sun and moon, but sometimes the sun and moon were eclipsed, and what should she do about the eclipse? She said she was able to meditate on a lake, but sometimes waves would appear, and what should she do about the waves? The meaning of her questions, of course, was that she was able to meditate on mind, but when she did this thoughts would arise, and how could she meditate on these thoughts?

Milarepa replied that it was very good that she could meditate like the sky with the absence of any center or limit. When clouds appeared, one should not see them as being any different from the sky because they are just a manifestation of the sky. If one can realize and understand that the nature of these clouds is the sky, they will naturally disappear. If one is able to meditate on the mountain, that is good. The plants and trees growing on the mountain are not any different from the mountain; they are simply manifestations of the mountain. If one is able to meditate on the sun and moon, that is good and an eclipse of the sun or moon is nothing other than the nature of the sun and moon. If one is able to meditate on a great lake, waves are likely to occur, which is just the movement of the lake and therefore only a manifestation of the lake because there are no waves that are not a part of the lake. Then Milarepa said that if one is able to meditate on the mind, then sometimes thoughts will appear. But these thoughts are just movements occurring in the mind. They are nothing other than the mind, a manifestation of the mind. When one does not understand the nature of the thoughts, they are like waves upon the lake, but still part of the lake. When one understands the nature of thoughts and that they do not have any true essence, they will naturally be pacified. So one needs to understand that thoughts are not separate from the mind.

In this way Milarepa taught the union of śamatha and vipaśyanā. Resting without thoughts is śamatha meditation and seeing that these thoughts are nothing other than a manifestation of the mind is vipaśyanā meditation.

The Result of the Union

The union of śamatha and vipaśyanā is greater than achieving either śamatha or vipaśyanā, and this result is called genuine samādhi. When one has genuine samādhi, the meditative and postmeditative periods are blended. So one practices meditation, then one arises from the meditation session and through familiarization with meditation, one can continue one's daily activities while resting in this state of meditation. So this blending of meditation and postmeditation is genuine samādhi—the union of śamatha and vipaśyanā.

The great translator Marpa brought teachings on meditation from India to Tibet. Marpa had two principal teachers—Nāropa and Maitrīpa. From Nāropa he learned the path of methods in which there are various methods to be practiced to gain realization. But Maitrīpa's teaching emphasizes direct meditation, which is also very important. This teaching can be found in the *Commentary on the Ten Suchnesses*. In this text he said that genuine samādhi will accomplish a result. This means that the union of śamatha and vipaśyanā is the greatest thing one can achieve. There is nothing higher than this because what needs to be realized has been realized and what needs to be eliminated has been eliminated. The samādhi with the union of śamatha and vipaśyanā fully developed will free one from the bondage of saṃsāra so one attains a state of nonabiding nirvāṇa, which is Buddhahood.

Some people are very fond of studying the dharma

and practicing meditation, but are not interested in achieving Buddhahood. They believe Buddhahood is opposed to worldliness and that to achieve Buddhahood is to somehow depart from this world and go to some buddha-realm or paradise. But achieving Buddhahood is not that at all. The Tibetan word for "Buddha" is *sang-gye; sang* means "clear," and *gye* means "increased" or "developed." The main syllable of this word is *gye,* "developed," but the translators wanted to make the meaning of the Buddha really clear, so they added the first syllable, *sang.* Through this samādhi of the union of śamatha and vipaśyanā one is able to remove all the faults of the kleśas and develop complete understanding of the nature of phenomena. One therefore becomes clear of these defects, which is the meaning of the syllable *sang.* Once all the kleśas have been eliminated, all the wisdom and positive qualities of the Buddha develop and this is the meaning of the syllable *gye.* Buddhahood isn't the act of going to a pure realm, but rather being in the ordinary world with the achievement of the union of śamatha and vipaśyanā.

The sūtra of the *Explanation of the View* says that through śamatha and vipaśyanā one becomes free of the bondage of the negative propensities. We are now in the human realm, which is one of the three higher realms (the god realm, jealous god realm, and human realm), but if the mind poisons are present this will result in accumulating negative karma, and accumulating negative karma will result in being reborn in one of the lower realms (the animal realm, hungry ghost realm, and hell realm). When one becomes free of the kleśas, one also becomes free from the bondage of conceptual designations. For the ordinary person, the mind grasps at things and is so attached to phenomena that it doesn't see their true nature. So the bondage of negative propensities prevents the development of meditation, the elimination of the kleśas, the rebirth in a higher realm, and the attainment of liberation. The bondage of negative propensities and the bondage of conceptual characteristics (described in the *Explanation of the View* sūtra) are the obscurations of the kleśas and the obscurations of knowledge. When these obscurations are removed, all the positive qualities such as wisdom, clairvoyance, and miraculous powers naturally appear. This is similar to when the clouds move away from in front of the sun so that the sun shines in its full brilliance without anything new having to be created. In the same way, clearing away all the obscurations allows all the positive qualities to shine in their brilliance.

In brief, we sit in meditation and focus our mind upon the external inseparability of appearance and emptiness and the internal inseparability of awareness and emptiness. Then if we allow our mind to become involved in many different thoughts in the postmeditation state, we will not be able to make any progress in our meditation. So we need to have mindfulness and awareness in the postmeditation state. In the beginning this is difficult, but whatever we are doing we should use mindfulness to control our awareness so that a natural control of our actions is developed. When we are working, eating, going somewhere, or talking with someone, we cultivate this natural self-control of mindfulness and awareness. The text says that in postmeditation we see all phenomena as being illusory. This means that in postmeditation we retain whatever reality and understanding we have gained in our meditation and see all phenomena as illusion so that we won't become attached to phenomena. This is what we should do in the post-meditative state.

There are three kinds of behavior that one should practice in the postmeditative state: (1) making offerings to the Buddhas and bodhisattvas, (2) developing compassion toward beings, and (3) dedicating all of one's good actions and karma. One makes offerings to the Buddhas and bodhisattvas not because offerings make them happy and once happy they will help us. One makes offerings because the dharma is very important and the practice of dharma is special. The Buddha is the one who taught the dharma and the bodhisattvas are special beings who have been able to practice the dharma without obstacles. Making offerings to these special beings increases one's own motivation to practice the dharma and to meditate. Without the development of genuine meditation one will remain in saṃsāra and experience suffering, being continuously reborn. But if one has genuine meditation one will attain liberation. One must develop compassion toward other beings because they are suffering. They are suffering because they haven't been able to develop genuine meditation. So by making an offering to the Buddhas and bodhisattvas and developing compassion toward beings, this becomes part of one's own aspiration and interest in the development of samādhi. Through the development of one's samādhi, one will be able to help other beings.

One also makes a vast dedication, which means dedicating to all beings whatever realization and experience one has acquired from one's meditation or whatever good karma one has accumulated.[13] Does this mean that when one does a good action, then one can give it to someone else? No, because when one does a good deed, one receives the result of that action and can't give one's good karma to others. But there is a dedication prayer dedicating one's actions to others, so isn't it rather pointless? Let us take an example. Say we wanted a flower to grow on this table before us. No matter how hard we pray, no flower will grow there. To have a flower grow on the table, we must get a flower pot, soil, water, and the proper seed. In the same way, by making dedication prayers, we develop a strong motivation to help others, then through the good karma that we accumulate from this, we will be able to help beings. So if we dedicate our good actions, they will never be wasted because eventually our wish will be fulfilled. That is why we should do a vast dedication to all beings in our postmeditation.

Different Kinds of Śamatha

The next section of the *Treasury of Knowledge* is a review of the different kinds of śamatha and vipaśyanā. Beginning with śamatha, there is the śamatha of the general yānas and then there is the śamatha specific to the vajarayāna. Śamatha of the sūtra method consists of śamatha meditation on the nine kinds of unpleasantness as a remedy for desire, on love and compassion as a remedy for anger, and on the breath as a remedy for too many thoughts.

The śamatha of the vajrayāna uses a number of methods. The vajrayāna is often better because it has many different kinds of methods that make the path much easier to practice. Thus, there are a variety of methods such as the meditation on love in which one develops the wish that beings have happiness. If beings are without happiness, one wishes that they can become happy and can have the conditions that bring happiness. This is the meditation on love, which is directed at all beings. Through this meditation on love one develops and increases one's śamatha meditation, which itself increases one's meditation on love. Then one meditates on those who are suffering and wishes that they be free from suffering and the causes of suffering. This meditation on compassion increases one's meditation, which increases one's compassion. So in this way, developing love and compassion increases the stability and stillness of one's mind.

The method for developing love and compassion is to first meditate on the sameness of oneself and others. One thinks that everything one experiences that is pleasurable is what other beings also like. If one experiences things one does not like, it is the same for other beings. In this way one contemplates and realizes the sameness of oneself and others. Next one meditates on cherishing others more than oneself. There are actions one does for oneself. If one does this for other beings instead of acting just for oneself, it is of much greater benefit. So others are seen as more important than oneself. Finally, there is the practice of exchanging oneself for others, known as sending and taking (Tib. *tonglen*). Through this practice one's mind poisons become less and one's love and compassion for others increase, and the stability of one's mind increases.

There is also the vajrayāna practice of breathing used within the Kagyü tradition called gentle breathing in three phases. In normal breathing, there is an in-breath and an out-breath. In this practice of breathing one counts the inhalation and exhalation of the breath to develop stability of mind. The *Treasury of Knowledge* mentions the in-breath, out-breath, and the pause between these when the breath remains in the body. This is Gampopa's "gentle breath practice in three stages." This method is not like "vase breathing," which is a stronger and more intense method, too strong for the beginner. In Gampopa's method first there is the in-breath, then the breath is held at the abdomen for a while, and then there is the out-breath, making three different stages. The reason for holding the breath is that normal breathing is done at the level of the mouth and the breath does not spread throughout the body. However, if one holds the breath, then the air will spread throughout the body. If one holds the breath at the level of the chest, one does not get the air through the body and it feels uncomfortable. If one holds the breath below the area of the navel, the air will spread throughout the body.

If one meditates just on inhalation and exhalation, it is possible to become distracted and forget one's meditation. If one's meditation is on inhalation, holding the breath, and exhalation, then if one loses one's mindfulness one will forget to hold the breath and it will be obvious that one has lost one's awareness. So doing breathing in three stages is more beneficial to develop stability of mind than just meditating on the in- and out-breath.

The first method specific to the vajrayāna is the method called individual withdrawal (Skt. *pratyahāra,* Tib. *sordu*), which involves cutting through the objects of mind. There are six obstacles that are the principal obstacles to śamatha meditation. These are dullness, agitation, aggression, regret, uncertainty, and attachment. One has to recognize each of these obstacles individually. In meditation one can investigate each of these. One might think, for example, "I'm feeling regret. This is an obstacle so I have to apply the remedy to it." It is easier to take one particular kind of thought or obstacle and deal with that, rather than deal with all thoughts as they come up. This is called the individual withdrawal because the "individual" refers to the individual obstacles that are cut through.

The second śamatha practice of the vajrayāna is called the empty structure of channels (*nādīs*). In the body there are three principal channels—the central channel (*avadūti*), the left channel (*lolanā*), and the right channel (*rasana*). In this practice one meditates on these three channels and the chakras.

The third method is the practice of prāṇa yoga or the practice of the vayūs (subtle airs in the body). One's meditation is on the subtle channels and one meditates on the subtle airs that flow through the channels. There are different yogas and practices for these subtle airs. There is a practice for bringing long life and there's a practice for making the body feel blissful and there is the practice for increasing wisdom, and so on. Then there is the practice of the bindus or subtle drops where one makes the bindus permeate the body, creating physical bliss and the experience of the union of bliss and emptiness.

In the vajrayāna teachings there is also the practice of meditation on the yidam deities. Sometimes one imagines the yidam above one's head and sometimes one imagines oneself as the yidam deity. Sometimes to make one's meditation on the deity clearer, one meditates on letters and syllables of a mantra. They are at times imagined as very large and sometimes very small, but all this is in order to create stability of mind. Through this visualization or development phase of practice one is able to eliminate the impure appearances of phenomena and develop pure appearances. By inviting the wisdom deities one receives the blessing. The visualization practice is a special method for developing a stability of mind that is not too tight or too loose. One just rests in the natural state of the mind. In general, the visualization (Tib. *kyerim*) stage of the practices act as methods for developing śamatha meditation. Some people do visualization practices with the hope of getting a very clear visualization. When this does not happen, they become disappointed and do not like to do the practice. It is not the purpose of the visualization to get a clear visualization, but to meditate on the nature of the deity so one can develop its pure appearances and create stability of mind. When one becomes distracted, the deity will be forgotten and one will readily notice it. Therefore, visualization is a special means to develop stability of mind and awareness.

Sometimes when we become tired of visualizing a deity or meditating on our breath, we can then do mantra recitation practice. Reciting mantras can be done with a sound or without a sound. When we recite a mantra without a sound, we do it quietly so that no one can hear it. It is traditionally described as reciting the mantra "so that the sound only reaches one's collar." When reciting the mantra we should be aware of each syllable of the mantra so the mind is aware of each of these syllables. If the mantra is OM MANI PEME HUNG we don't just recite it without being aware of it, but recite it very quietly, so that others can barely hear it, keeping the mind aware of the sound of the mantra without distraction. There is also the mental recitation of the mantra in which we do not use our voice. We count the mantras with our *mālā* and recite the mantra fully in our mind. We usually do one hundred of these and there is no possibility of being distracted by mentally reciting the mantra because we are counting on the *mālā*. Doing this makes our mind stable and it also makes the mind's orientation to the mantra become much clearer.

Then there is mantra recitation called recitation with cessation. The mental recitation is joined to the breathing so that it is not just a mental recitation. We recite one part of the mantra while inhaling, one part while holding the breath, and one part while exhaling. This does not involve actual sound. For example, with the Guru Rinpoche (Padmasambhava) mantra, on the in-breath we recite OM ĀH HUNG and with the held breath we recite BENDZA GURU PEMA and with the out-breath SIDDHI HUNG. The reason this is called recitation with cessation is that this method stops all thoughts.

There are the above methods that use a reference point, and there is also the method of direct or naked recognition of the mind's nature. All these methods are means to develop supreme wisdom. There are many methods to gain this wisdom and the methods are given in accordance with the individual's capabilities and nature. Some methods are for individuals with strong devotion, some are for those with strong understanding, and so on, so one doesn't do every method of śamatha and vipaśyanā described, but the one that is suitable to one's capacity and nature.

The Union of Śamatha & Vipaśyanā

What is developed by all the practices of śamatha is stability of mind. With this stability one can develop vipaśyanā. If the mind is stable and resting in its natural state, one can use sharp understanding to analyze and investigate the texts or understand the meaning of the words of the texts. So with stability of mind, one can examine and understand whatever one focuses one's mind on, so that one's śamatha practice becomes vipaśyanā practice.

Sometimes analytical meditation is done by itself and sometimes nonanalytic meditation is done alone. Sometimes they are done alternately. If done correctly, either method can lead to the development of śamatha and vipaśyanā. In terms of a goal they are the same; in terms of a path, however, there is a difference between them.

Levels and Results of Meditation

The text gives an added explanation of the three different levels of meditation (dhyāna). The first level is of ordinary beings and this is called literally *the experience of an immature being.* In terms of practice, the person at this level is able to recognize to a certain extent when a distraction occurs and is able to return to meditation. Through doing this, various experiences of meditation occur. The second stage is the level of the bodhisattva and this is called the level of *meditation that differentiates meanings.* In this meditative state there is a very clear understanding of the nature of phenomena such as dependent origination, the illusory nature of phenomena, and so on and wisdom develops more and more. The third state is *the ultimate stage of a Buddha* in which the nature of phenomena is seen; this is known as the primordial nature of peace. It is not a new wisdom, but a realization that comes completely effortlessly. So these are the three kinds of meditation in relation to "thatness, the true nature of phenomena."

The *Treasury of Knowledge* does not discuss the experiences that come from meditation in particular, so I shall offer my own thoughts on this topic as a summary.

The result of practicing meditation is realization and experience. Meditation experiences are temporary and come rather quickly. Realization, however, is attained through the gradual process of meditation and is lasting. One has to work on attaining realization, whereas one should have no attachment to the experience of meditation whether good or bad. If one has a good experience in meditation, one should think that it is just an appearance or manifestation of the mind and have no joy that one has had it. If one does develop an attachment to meditational experiences, one will develop pride, which will cause further obstacles to one's meditation. If one has a bad experience, one should not be frightened because it also is just an appearance of mind.

The different experiences of meditation are due to the differences of the subtle channels. Some people get experiences right away, others don't get any particular meditational experience until their meditation becomes firm and stable. There is no reason to feel happy that one has had a good experience or think that one is not getting anywhere because one has had no experiences. There is also no reason to think that one has a problem because one is having different experiences in meditation, or that one does not have stable meditation because one is having few or no experiences. There is no reason to be happy or sad because experiences in meditation are just a creation of the mind due to different kinds of channels and have nothing to do with meditation.

There are three kinds of meditation experiences—bliss, clarity, and the absence of thoughts. The experience of bliss occurs when one is meditating and feels happy and has a feeling of physical bliss. If this occurs, one should have no attachment to it or take it as a sign of good meditation. Instead one should just ignore it and keep on with the meditation. There is a very clear awareness in which one sees everything and knows everything with the experience of clarity and this is also just a fabrication of mind. One should not think that this is genuine meditation but should have no attachment or involvement in this experience of clarity. When one experiences the absence of thought, one may think that one has attained a state of complete stability in meditation. But one shouldn't stop there, one should just continue unceasingly with one's practice of meditation.

When one is practicing the dharma and there are no great obstacles, it is easy to develop internal obstacles to one's practice. This occurs because one begins to think that one has a great practice and feels very proud. This pride itself is a great obstacle to one's dharma practice and meditation. It is said in Tibet that "into the solid ball of pride the water of positive qualities cannot be poured." This means that when one becomes proud, one is like a solid lump and this becomes an obstacle. Instead one should have humility, faith, and devotion to the dharma. Because pride is such a great obstacle, one should examine oneself to see if pride is there or not.

When Gampopa first heard the name "Milarepa," he felt great faith in Milarepa and went to find him. He kept asking the way until he finally got very close to where Milarepa was staying. The pupils of Milarepa came out to meet him, and one of his students, a woman, said she would take him to her house to stay the night and the next day she would take him to see Milarepa. She said that she had seen Milarepa that day and Milarepa had told her that there would be a monk coming from central Tibet who had good qualities and would be a great pupil of his. Milarepa had also said that the one who introduced this monk to Milarepa would be very fortunate and would not be reborn in the lower realms. After hearing this, Gampopa thought, "Oh, if Milarepa is a great siddha, he has great knowledge. From the way he talked I am very fortunate and will not have much difficulty with dharma practice." Gampopa became so proud that Milarepa sent down a pupil each day for two weeks saying, "Don't be upset, but you can't come to see Milarepa yet." In this way, Gampopa's pride was eliminated. So we see how pride can be an obstacle to dharma practice.

Some individuals who practice in a very dark retreat (*bardo* retreat) will see all sorts of lights and will feel their bodies shaking and so on during meditations. These are experiences that one must not become attached to because they are just appearances of the mind. Good or bad, one just continues with one's meditation without becoming involved with them. Since dreams are expressions of the mind, the meditation will create all kinds of dreams. But there is no need to become attached to a good dream or fixated upon a bad dream. For example, when Gampopa went to see Milarepa to tell him about his various dreams, Milarepa replied, "You were lying to me when you came and said that you had done a lot of practice. If you had done a lot of practice, you wouldn't have all this attachment to dreams."

If one has a dream and thinks something good is going to happen but nothing actually happens in one's practice, then one will lose the determination to practice. Similarly, if one experiences bliss and clarity in one's meditation and thinks, "Oh, I have a very good meditation" and becomes attached to it, but the next time one does not experience it, one might then think, "Oh, I have lost my meditation." So one should not be attached to these experiences, but realize that these experiences do not change the essence of one's meditation. Even if one doesn't experience anything, one does not change one's meditation but just practices with that state of mind in meditation.

Posture of the body is very important in meditation. For example, when Gampopa was practicing, he had the experience of the whole valley outside his cave becoming filled with smoke. When the smoke cleared, he became very uncomfortable because he heard great shouting. He thought that he must have become afflicted by some kind of demon or spirit. When he asked Milarepa about it, Milarepa replied that his posture was not correct and this was tightening his inner channels, which then caused these experiences. So the seven aspects of the Vairocana posture or the five aspects of dhyāna posture are important. It is not essential to have one's legs in the vajra posture, but it is very important to have one's body sitting very straight. This sitting up straight is important whether one is reciting a mantra, doing a visualization, or practicing any other kind of meditation. Sitting upright enables one to have mindfulness, awareness, and attentiveness to one's meditation practice and the vayūs will flow correctly in the subtle channels.

To meditate we need to have the great diligence called armor-like diligence. It is like armor because when we wear armor, we have great courage. The reason we need this diligence is because the vajrayāna teaches how to attain Buddhahood in one lifetime, and when people hear this they have the expectation of reaching the goal very quickly. When they don't get great results quickly, they then lose confidence. So we need to have great diligence without the expectation of achieving quick results because first we have to eliminate all the mind poisons to which we have become habituated throughout beginningless saṃsāra. Then we have to attain all the qualities, wisdom, and omniscience of the Buddha. In order to attain these positive qualities and eliminate all the negative mind poisons, we need great diligence. So we must not think that there will be quick results to our practice. We can achieve Buddhahood within one lifetime in the vajrayāna, but we need a great deal of diligence like that of Milarepa, which is difficult for most people to muster.

We might think that we will achieve Buddhahood if we have great diligence like Milarepa and that nothing will happen by doing just a little bit each day. We might think, "I don't have Milarepa's diligence, so it is impossible for me to achieve any results." We shouldn't believe that without great diligence it won't make any difference if we practice dharma or not. The Buddha said that doing any meditation is very good. For example, he said that even if someone just has the thought of where he is going to go and what he is going to do, even though he has not yet arrived there or done anything, it will bring a beneficial result. Similarly, a result will come from just thinking of future practice. Generally speaking, just taking a couple of steps to where one is going to meditate has no benefit in itself but according to the Buddha it does eventually bring a beneficial result. So our meditation practice is very beneficial and we should not think that there is no point or purpose in doing meditation because we don't have the kind of diligence that Milarepa had.

It is important to continue steadily with our meditation practice rather than have intense periods of diligence and then give it up because there is no result. This kind of diligence is called unchanging, permanent diligence that enables us to maintain the continuity of our practice. We need this kind of diligence. It is important both to have this diligence and not to have any attachment to meditation experiences.

Notes

1. All Tibetan words are spelled phonetically. The transliterations for these words are given in the table on pages 158–60.
2. The word for "meditation" in Tibetan is transliterated as *sgom* (Skt. *bhāvanā*) and pronounced *gom*. The word for "habituate" is *goms* (Skt. *abhyāsa*), pronounced *khom*. These words are similar in Tibetan because the *s* is silent.
3. This word is translitered as *zhi gnas* in Tibetan and is often spelled *shi-ne* in English. It is pronounced "she-*nay*."
4. Some scholars believe that Hashang Mahāyāna's teaching was connected with Zen Buddhism. I do not believe so. In the Tibetan texts there is no description of Hashang Mahāyāna's teaching. A number of Tibetans say it was the Chinese tradition that spread to China, but I believe that it was something particular to Hashang Mahāyāna. *Hashang Mahāyāna* is an individual's name, whereas *Hashang* is a general name of a person in the dharma tradition. The history of the sixteen arhats in Tibet says that they were together and did many miracles and that their patron was Hashang. Also, some scholars describe *Hashang* as a symbol for the *ālaya,* or ground consciousness. There are six consciousnesses, which can be compared to six children who are a bother because they are running around all the time. Imagine an old man sitting with six children jumping about, never giving him any peace. So you have Hashang sitting there with all these children climbing all over him, but he is sitting there smiling and peaceful. This is a symbol for the ground consciousness being unperturbed by the six consciousnesses. In this way Hashang is a symbol.

There is also another Hashang in Tibetan history. He is

called Hashang who is depicted iconographically as carrying a big sack with him. He was a teacher and an emanation of Maitreya who spread the dharma in China. This Hashang Maitreya looks like the Hashang who is with the sixteen arhats. He is, however, completely different from the Hashang Mahāyāna monk who came to Tibet to teach meditation.

5. There are several kinds of subtle airs or winds, called *vayūs* in Sanskrit. There is the vayū of air or vayū of fire. It makes the body warm and provides the heat and well-being of the body. The vayū of the element fire provides the warmth of the body. The vayū of the element water keeps the body moist, pervades the whole body, and has the function of the element of water. The vayū of the element of air provides for the physical movement of the body. The ability to move and the suppleness of the body come from the vayū (air) of the air element. The movements of both the mind and the body come through this vayū. The vayū of earth provides the stability of the body and keeps the body from going into a state of change. It gives the body physical solidity. In this way the commentaries talk of the "air of earth," the "air of air," and so on.

In general there are four elements: earth, fire, air, and water. Earth is the ground beneath us, water is the material that flows downward, fire is what burns, and air (the Tibetan word for which also means "wind") is what moves around us. The earth element has the aspect of solidity and durability. The fire element has the aspect of warmth and burning. The water element has the aspect of moistness. The air element has the aspect of movement. These four qualities of solidity, warmth, moistness, and movement are what is meant by the four elements. The functions of the elements are, for example, that the earth makes something very solid and durable and the water element causes cohesion and keeps things together. For instance, a finger just doesn't disintegrate; it stays together in one piece, and this is the function of the water element. The function of the fire element is ripening, causing things to change. For example, it is the aspect of warmth that causes a flower to develop. Things develop, mature, and go into a state of decline and aging, and the entire process of change is due to the activity of the fire element.

6. Some centers do walking meditation between sitting meditation periods. During walking meditation there is no particular visualization. One should be aware of each foot as it goes up, then goes down, and so forth. One is simply aware of the walking movement, a process similar to resting on the breath. This method is used in the Theravādin tradition and is described in the vinaya texts. In Tibet, however, most meditation was traditionally done sitting down. I think walking meditation can be very beneficial because it is good for the mind, is good for the body, and doesn't hurt the knees.

7. These times are purely illustrative and should not be taken literally.

8. To be more precise, emptiness is *śūnyatā* (Tib. *tongpanyi*), knowledge is *vidya (rigpa),* the union of emptiness and knowledge is *vidyaśunyasambheda (riktong yerme),* and clarity is *bhasvara (selwa).*

9. There is a difference in the understanding of emptiness depending on whether one uses the hīnayāna or the mahāyāna viewpoint. According to Chandrakīrti, the only difference between these two is the degree of realization and the greater number of practices that one does in the mahāyāna. The quality of the understanding of emptiness is the same. In the beginning of his work *Entering into the Middle Way,* Chandrakīrti writes that there is little difference. However, toward the end of the text he talks about the two kinds of selflessness: the selflessness of individuals, such as is realized by śrāvakas, and the selflessness of phenomena in the mahāyāna. So there are two different viewpoints among the Tibetans on what this means. Some say that according to Chandrakīrti the śrāvakas do realize the emptiness of phenomena. Others interpret this to say that śrāvakas do not realize the emptiness of phenomena, only the selflessness of the individual. So there is a difference on this point among

Tibetan scholars. I believe that śrāvakas do not realize the selflessness of phenomena. I base this on studying the *Madhyamakāvatāra* using the commentary by Lama Mipam, which says that the śrāvakas don't realize the selflessness of phenomena. For example, Tsongkapa disagreed with this view, while the eighth Karmapa, Mikyo Dorje, for example, says that śrāvakas do not realize the selflessness of phenomena.

Once a person has reached Buddhahood, he or she has clarity, knowing everything is emptiness. One can't really look and find this wisdom, this clarity, but the power of the mind is still there. This wisdom is called *jñāna* in Sanskrit or *yeshe* in Tibetan. So there is this jñāna, or perfect wisdom, and then there is also love and power. The love has power because it is love with power, not like the love, for example, of a mother who has no arms and is trying to save her child who is being swept away by a strong current.

One may ask if the dharma itself is also empty. The answer is that dharma teachings do not have the nature of true existence in themselves. When one receives dharma teachings, one benefits from them only if one puts them into practice. Receiving teachings without practicing is just hearing words, or if they are written down, it is just black ink on white paper. So they have no value by themselves. Taking another example, what makes a precious human existence valuable? The human body by itself has little value, but when it is put to use, it can have great value. The commentaries refer to the teachings as being like a boat. The boats in the old days were made out of leather, and these were not very valuable. But the value of a boat is that with it one can cross over to the other side of a river. In the same way, dharma and precious human existence are valuable—they have no value in themselves, but one gains great value from them when one uses them.

10. One might wonder about emptiness and awareness at the time of total liberation. Buddhahood is called liberation, and this is not like something one gets or achieves that one did not have before. Liberation is the realization of the actual

nature of phenomena without any contrivance. Because one doesn't realize the natural state of phenomena, one is in a state of delusion believing in what doesn't exist. Once one realizes this natural state, then one has attained liberation from saṃsāra. To do this, one first analyzes phenomena through reasoning. Through this analysis one attains the understanding of the true nature of phenomena. But even though one has this understanding, one still is not familiarized with or habituated to it. So one needs to become habituated to the true nature of phenomena before one has attained complete liberation.

Tilopa asked, "Where is the sesame oil?" The sesame oil is in the sesame seeds, but one doesn't get any sesame oil by simply eating sesame seeds. To get sesame oil, one has to beat, grind, or crush the seeds. It is like that with Buddhahood: it is within one, but in order to achieve liberation one has to apply oneself to meditation to realize it. Another example of liberation is the analogy of the rope and the snake. If there is a rope in a poorly lit room and one sees it, one might think that it is a snake, and the result will be great fear. This fear arises because of the illusion that the rope is a snake. To be free of that fear, one has to realize that the snake is really a rope, and no other solution such as getting a weapon or taking an antidote to the snake venom is going to work. When one does realize that the snake is just a rope, then all the fear naturally disappears. This happens even though there was absolutely no change in the rope either before or after. The only difference was that before one was deluded, and afterward one discovered the truth. So to achieve the complete peace of mind of Buddhahood, one has to receive the teachings, follow the methods taught by the Buddha, and contemplate them, thereby removing the delusions and attaining the realization of the true nature of the mind.

11. This painting is a large circle divided into six pie-shaped segments depicting the six realms of existence: the god, jealous god, human, animal, hungry ghost, and hell realms.

12. In more detail, there is the Tibetan term *yeshe* (Skt. *jñāna*), which has been translated as "wisdom" in this book. In Sanskrit *jñāna* is not a particularly special word and simply means "to know." When the Tibetan translators translated *jñāna* into Tibetan, they added the syllable *ye* to *she* because *ye* means "primordial knowledge that has always existed." This word was then used for the knowledge of the Buddha, who knows all things in their ultimate and relative aspects. The Tibetan word *sherab*, or *prajñā* in Sanskrit, has been translated as "understanding" in this book. The syllable *she* means "to know," and the syllable *rab* means "the best, superior to everything, perfect" in Tibetan. The terms *sherab* and *yeshe* are often used interchangeably as "knowledge" and "wisdom." But one can differentiate between them, because *yeshe* is the knowledge a Buddha or enlightened being has, which is the direct understanding of phemonena, whereas *sherab* is the understanding one gains through analysis, examination, and reasoning. *Sherab* is related to the differentiation of phenomena. In one's normal experience, all phenomena are merged together, and through the understanding of *sherab* all phenomena are differentiated so that one knows this is this, that is that, this exists, that doesn't, this is good, that is bad, and so on. So all phenomena are differentiated from each other, and this is the special meaning of *sherab*. The knowledge in meditation where one knows the true nature of things is *rigpa* in Tibetan or *vidya* in Sanskrit. So this clarity, the knowledge of the true nature of things, is called *rigpa*.

13. The dedication prayer is said by the lamas and their students usually at the end of each dharma teaching as well as at any sādhana practices:

> Through this merit may omniscience be attained;
> Thereby may every enemy [mental defilements] be
>   overcome.
> May beings be liberated from the ocean of saṃsāra,
> Which is troubled by the waves of birth, sickness, old
>   age, and death.

Glossary

Many of the terms in this glossary have several different meanings. The definitions given here are those that are relevant to the context of this book.

ABHIDHARMA (Tib. *chö ngönpa*) The Buddhist teachings are often divided into the Tripiṭaka: the sūtras (teachings of the Buddha), the vinaya (teachings on conduct), and the abhidharma, which are the analyses of phenomena that exist primarily as a commentarial tradition to the Buddhist teachings. There is not, in fact, an abhidharma section within the Tibetan collection of the Buddhist teachings.

AFFLICTED CONSCIOUSNESS See consciousnesses, eight.

AGGREGATES, FIVE (Skt. *skandha*, Tib. *pungpo nga*) Literally, "heaps"; the five basic transformations that perceptions undergo when an object is perceived. First is form, which includes all sounds, smells, etc., or everything that is not mind. The second and third are sensations (pleasant and unpleasant, etc.) and identification. Fourth is mental events, which actually include the second and third aggregates. The fifth is ordinary consciousness such as the sensory and mental consciousnesses.

ĀLAYA CONSCIOUSNESS (Tib. *künshi namshe*) According to the Yogāchārā school this is the eighth consciousness and is often called the ground consciousness or storehouse consciousness.

AMṚITA (Tib. *dutsi*) A blessed substance that can cause spiritual and physical healing.

ARHAT (Tib. *dra chompa*) Accomplished hīnayāna practitioners who have eliminated the kleśas. They are fully realized śrāvakas and pratyekabuddhas.

Glossary

AVALOKITEŚVARA (Tib. *Chenrezi*)   Deity of compassion.

ĀYATANA (Tib. *kyemeh*)   The six sense consciousnesses and their sensory objects.

BARDO (Tib. *bardo*)   Literally, "between the two." There are six kinds of bardos, but in this book the term refers to the time between death and rebirth.

BARDO RETREAT   An advanced vajrayāna practice in which the practitioner is enclosed in total darkness.

BINDU (Tib. *tig-le*)   Vital essence drops or spheres of psychic energy, often visualized in vajrayāna practices.

BODHISATTVA (Tib. *changchub sempa*)   An individual committed to the mahāyāna path of compassion and the practice of the six pāramitās to achieve Buddhahood in order to free all beings from saṃsāra.

BODHISATTVA VOW   A vow in which one promises to practice in order to bring all other sentient beings to Buddhahood.

BUDDHA ŚĀKYAMUNI   Often called the Gautama Buddha; refers to the latest Buddha who lived between 563 and 483 B.C.E.

CENTRAL CHANNEL (Skt. *avadhūti*; Tib. *uma*)   This is a subtle channel of the body roughly located along the spine.

CHAKRA   Literally, "wheels." These are points along the central channel specifically located at the forehead, throat, heart, etc., where there is a broadening of channels.

CHAKRAVARTIN (Tib. *khorlo gyurpa*)   Literally, "the turner of the wheel"; also called a universal monarch. This is a king who propagates the dharma and starts a new era.

CONDITIONED EXISTENCE   *See* saṃsāra.

CONSCIOUSNESSES, EIGHT   These include the five sensory consciousnesses of sight, hearing, smell, taste, and touch. The sixth is the mental consciousness; the seventh is afflicted consciousness; and the eighth is ground consciousness.

DAKA (Tib. *dapo*)   A wrathful or semiwrathful male yidam.

ḌĀKINĪ (Tib. *kandroma*)   A wrathful or semiwrathful female yidam.

Glossary

DEFINITIVE MEANING   Teachings of the Buddha that give the direct meaning of dharma and are not changed or simplified to accommodate the capacity of the listener. This contrasts with the provisional meaning.

DEPENDENT ORIGINATION (Skt. *pratītyasamutpāda*)   The twelve successive phases that begin with ignorance and end with old age and death.

DESIRE REALM   *See* realms, three.

DHARMA (Tib. *chö*)   This has two principal meanings: (1) any truth, such as "the sky is blue," (2) the teachings of the Buddha (also called buddhadharma).

DHARMADHĀTU (Tib. *chöying*)   The all-encompassing space that is unoriginated and beginningless from which all phenomena arise.

DHYĀNA MEDITATION (Tib. *sampten*)   The Sanskrit refers to "meditation," but in this context it refers to "mental stability" in relation to śamatha.

DOHĀ (Tib. *gur*)   A religious song spontaneously composed by a vajrayāna practitioner, usually consisting of nine syllables per line.

FORM REALM   See realms, three.

FORMLESS REALM   See realms, three.

GROUND CONSCIOUSNESS   See consciousnesses, eight.

GURU YOGA   The practice of devotion to the guru culminating in receiving his blessing and blending indivisibly with him. It is the fourth practice of the preliminary practices.

HĪNAYĀNA (Tib. *tekpa chungwa*)   Literally, "the lesser vehicle." The term refers to the first teachings of the Buddha, which emphasized the careful examination of mind and its confusion; also called the Theravādin path.

INDIVIDUAL ABSORPTION OR WITHDRAWAL (Skt. *pratyā-hāra*)   This is the first stage of the completion phase of practice.

INSIGHT MEDITATION   *See* vipaśyanā meditation.

JÑĀNA (Tib. *yeshe*)   Enlightened wisdom that is beyond dualistic thought.

Glossary

KAGYÜ   One of the four major schools of Buddhism in Tibet. It was founded by Marpa and is headed by His Holiness Karmapa. The other three schools are the Nyingma, the Sākya, and the Gelug.

KARMA (Tib. *lay*)   Literally, "action." Karma is a universal law ensuring that when one does a wholesome action, one's circumstances will improve, and when one does an unwholesome action, negative results will eventually occur from the act.

KLEŚA (Tib. *nyönmong*)   The emotional obscurations (in contrast to intellectual obscurations), usually translated as "poisons" or "defilements." The three main kleśas are ignorance, hatred, and desire. The five kleśas include these three along with pride and envy.

KUSULU   Said to be a combination of the first syllables for eating, sleeping, and moving around. It means one who leads a very simple life dedicated to meditation and not scholastic studies and elaborate rituals.

LAMA (Skt. *guru*)   A teacher in the Tibetan tradition who has reached realization.

LEFT CHANNEL (Skt. *lalanā*)   This subtle channel is parallel to the central channel and is usually visualized as white. The left, central, and right channels are the three principal channels within the body that conduct the subtle airs.

MĀDHYAMAKA   A philosophical school founded by Nāgārjuna in the second century. The main principle of this school is proving through analytical reasoning that everything is empty of self-nature.

MAHĀMUDRĀ (Tib. *chagya chenpo*)   Literally, "great seal" or "great symbol." This meditative transmission emphasizes perceiving mind directly rather than through skillful means.

MAHĀYĀNA (Tib. *tekpa chenpo*)   Literally, "great vehicle." These are the teachings of the second turning of the Wheel of Dharma that were first taught at Vulture Peak Mountain by the Buddha and emphasized śūnyatā, compassion, and universal buddha-nature.

MAHĀPAṆḌITA   A very great Buddhist scholar (*paṇḍita*).

Glossary

MĀLĀ   A rosary of beads used for mantra practice. A mālā usually has 108 beads.

MANTRA (Tib. *ngak*)   Invocations to various meditation deities that are recited in Sanskrit. These Sanskrit syllables, representing various energies, are repeated in different vajrayāna practices.

MANTRAYĀNA   Another term for the vajrayāna.

MAṆḌALA (Tib. *kyilkhor*)   A diagram used in various vajrayāna practices, usually depicting a central deity and four directions.

MENTAL CONSCIOUSNESS   *See* consciousnesses, eight.

NĀDĪ (Tib. *tsa*)   Subtle channels through which the subtle energy (*vayu*) flows.

NIRVĀṆA (Tib. *nya-ngen lay depa*)   Literally, "extinguished." State of enlightenment in which all false ideas and conflicting emotions have been extinguished.

NOBLE TRUTHS, FOUR (Tib. *pakpay denpa shi*)   These are the truth of suffering, the truth of the cause of suffering, the cessation of suffering, and the path. They are the foundation of Buddhism, particularly the hīnayāna path.

PĀRAMITĀS, SIX (Tib. *paröltu chinpa*)   Literally, "perfections." These are the six practices of the mahāyāna path: transcendent generosity (*dāna*), transcendent discipline (*śīla*), transcendent patience (*kṣānti*), transcendent exertion (*vīrya*), transcendent meditation (*dhyāna*), and transcendent wisdom (*prajñā*). The ten pāramitās are these plus the pāramitā of means, aspirational prayer, power, and pristine awareness.

PATH   The process of attaining enlightenment. *Path* may also refer to part of the threefold logic of ground, path, and fruition.

PATH OF METHODS (Tib. *tab lam*)   Practice emphasizing the techniques of the vajrayāna, particularly the six yogas of Nāropa.

POWA   An advanced tantric practice concerned with the ejection of consciousness at death.

PRAJÑĀ (Tib. *sherab*)   Literally, "perfect knowledge"; according to context, it can mean wisdom, understanding, intelligence, discrimination, or judgment. Here it refers to a higher kind of knowledge about phenomena.

Glossary

PRAJÑĀPĀRAMITĀ The Buddhist literature outlining the mahāyāna path and the teaching of emptiness.

PRĀṆA (Tib. *bindu*) Life-supporting energy.

PRĀTIMOKṢA VOWS (Tib. *sosortarpa*) The vows of conduct in the hīnayāna. There are seven main vows taken by lay persons and the ordained alike.

PRATYEKABUDDHA Literally, "solitary realizer." A realized hīnayāna practitioner who has achieved the jñāna of suchness and variety, but who has not committed him- or herself to the bodhisattva path of helping all other sentient beings.

PRELIMINARY PRACTICES (Tib. *ngöndro*) One usually begins the vajrayāna path by doing the four preliminary practices, which involve doing 100,000 refuge prostrations, 100,000 Vajrasattva mantras, 100,000 maṇḍala offerings, and 100,000 guru yoga supplications.

PROVISIONAL MEANING The teachings of the Buddha that have been simplified or modified to accommodate the capabilities of the audience. This contrasts with the definitive meaning.

REALMS, THREE The existence in saṃsāra is in one of three realms: the *desire realm* in which beings are reborn into the six realms of saṃsāra based on their karma; the *form realm* in which beings, due to the power of their meditation, are born with immaterial bodies; and the *formless realm* in which beings with meditative absorption have entered a state of meditation after death, where there are no bodies, no actual realms, or locations because all the processes of thought and perception have ceased.

RIGHT CHANNEL (Skt. *rasona*, Tib. *roma*) This subtle channel is parallel to the central channel and carries the vayū.

SĀDHANA (Tib. *drubtab*) A type of vajrayāna ritual text, as well as the actual meditation practice involved.

SAMĀDHI (Tib. *ting-ngen dzin*) Also called meditative absorption or one-pointed meditation; the highest form of meditation.

Glossary

ŚAMATHA MEDITATION (Tib. *shi-ne*) Also known as tranquillity meditation. This is basic sitting meditation in which one usually follows the breath while observing the workings of the mind.

SAMSĀRA (Tib. *khorwa*) Conditioned existence of ordinary life in which suffering occurs because one is still afflicted with ignorance, hatred, and desire. It is contrasted with nirvāṇa.

SAMSĀRA, SIX REALMS OF These consist of the god or deva realm, the jealous god or *asura* realm, the human realm, the animal realm, the hungry ghost or *preta* realm, and the hell realms.

SAṄGHA (Tib. *gendün*) These are the companions on the path. They may be all persons on the path or the holy realized ones.

ŚĀSTRA (Tib. *tenchö*) The Buddhist teachings are divided into words of the Buddha (sūtras) and the commentaries of others on his teachings (śāstras).

SENDING AND TAKING PRACTICE (Tib. *tonglen*) A meditation practice promulgated by Atiśa in which the practitioner takes on the negative conditions of others and gives out all that is positive.

SIDDHA (Tib. *drubtop*) An accomplished Buddhist practitioner.

ŚRĀVAKA (Tib. *nyentö*) Literally, "those who hear" meaning disciples. A type of realized hīnayāna practitioner (arhat) who has achieved the realization of the nonexistence of a self.

ŚŪNYATĀ (Tib. *tongpanyi*) Usually translated as "voidness" or "emptiness." The Buddha taught in the second turning of the Wheel of Dharma that external phenomena, internal phenomena, and the concept of self or "I" have no real existence and therefore are "empty."

SŪTRA (Tib. *do*) The hīnayāna and mahāyāna texts, which are the words of the Buddha. These are often contrasted with the tantras, which are the Buddha's vajrayāna teachings, and the śāstras, which are commentaries on the words of the Buddha.

TANTRA (Tib. *gyü*) The texts of the vajrayāna practices.

TATHĀGATAS Literally, "those who have gone to thusness." A title of the Buddha and bodhisattvas.

Glossary

TERTÖN   A master in the Tibetan tradition who discovers treasures (*terma*), which are teachings concealed by great masters of the past.

THERAVĀDA   A school derived from the early schools of Buddhism that primarily emphasized the hīnayāna teachings.

TIRTHIKAS   Religious people who believe in a personal self. Also referred to as icchantikas.

TRADITION OF PROFOUND VIEW   This tradition is one of the principal mahāyāna traditions in India, which was founded by Nāgārjuna in the second century A.D. It is the Mādhyamaka or "Middle Way" that teaches emptiness of all external and internal phenomena.

TRADITION OF VAST CONDUCT   This tradition is one of the two principal mahāyāna traditions in India founded by Asaṅga in the fourth century A.D. It is the Chittamatrin or "Mind Only" school that teaches how all phenomena are mind created. This gave rise to the mahāyāna traditions of abhidharma and logic.

THREE JEWELS   These are the Buddha, the dharma, and the saṅgha.

TRANQUILLITY MEDITATION   *See* śamatha meditation.

TÜLKU (Skt. *nirmānakāya*)   A manifestation of a buddha that is perceived by an ordinary person. The term has commonly been used for a discovered rebirth of any teacher.

UPĀYA   *See* path of methods.

VAJRA (Tib. *dorje*)   Usually translated "diamond-like." This may be an implement held in the hand during certain vajrayāna ceremonies or it may refer to a quality so pure and enduring that it is like a diamond.

VAJRAYĀNA (Tib. *dorje tekpa*)   There are three major traditions (or vehicles) of Buddhism: hīnayāna, mahāyāna, and vajrayāna). The vajrayāna, practiced mainly in Tibet, is based on the tantras and emphasizes the clarity aspect of phenomena.

VASE BREATHING   An advanced breathing practice that has to be learned under the supervision of an experienced teacher and involves the retention of the breath in the abdomen, which thus becomes like an air-filled vase.

VAYŪ (Tib. *lung*) In Sanskrit and Tibetan can mean "wind" outside or the air that is breathed as well as the subtle airs of the body. In this context it refers to the subtle airs or energies that travel along the subtle channels.

VINAYA (Tib. *dulwa*) These are the teachings by the Buddha concerning proper conduct.

VIPAŚYANĀ MEDITATION (Tib. *hlagtong*) Also known as insight meditation. A meditation practice that develops insight into the nature of mind. The other main meditation is śamatha meditation.

VISUAL CONSCIOUSNESS *See* consciousnesses, eight.

VISUALIZATION STAGE (Skt. *utpattikrama*) Also called developmental or generation phase. This is the practice of visualizing a yidam deity along with retinue, palace, mantra, etc.

YIDAM (Skt. *iṣṭadevatā*) A tantric deity that embodies qualities of Buddhahood used in the practice of vajrayāna.

Transliteration and Pronunciation
of Tibetan Terms

PRONOUNCED	SPELLED IN TIBETAN	TIBETAN
bardo	bar do	བར་དོ་
chagpa	chags pa	ཆགས་པ་
chagya chenpo	phyag rgya chen po	ཕྱག་རྒྱ་ཆེན་པོ་
changchub sempa	byang chub sems dpa'	བྱང་ཆུབ་སེམས་དཔའ་
changpa	sbyangs pa	སྦྱངས་པ་
Chenrezi	spyan ras gzigs	སྤྱན་རས་གཟིགས་
chö	chos	ཆོས་
chöying	chos dbyings	ཆོས་དབྱིངས་
chö ngönpa	chos mngon pa	ཆོས་མངོན་པ་
do	mdo	མདོ་
dorje	rdo rje	རྡོ་རྗེ་
dorje tekpa	rdo rje theg pa	རྡོ་རྗེ་ཐེག་པ་
drenpa	dranpa	དྲན་པ་
drubtop	grub thob	གྲུབ་ཐོབ་
dulwa	'dul ba	འདུལ་བ་

dutsi	bdud rtsi	བདུད་རྩི་
gendun	dge 'dun	དགེ་འདུན་
gom	sgom	སྒོམ་
gur	mgur	མགུར་
gyü	rgyud	རྒྱུད་
hlagthong	lhag mthong	ལྷག་མཐོང་
jangma	rkyang ma	རྐྱང་མ་
kandroma	mkha' 'gro ma	མཁའ་འགྲོ་མ་
khom	khoms	ཁོམས་
khorlo gyurwa	'khor lo bsgyur ba	འཁོར་ལོ་བསྒྱུར་བ་
khorwa	'khor ba	འཁོར་བ་
künshi namshe	kun gzhi rnam shes	ཀུན་གཞི་རྣམ་ཤེས་
kyeche	skye mched	སྐྱེ་མཆེད་
kyerim	bskyed rim	བསྐྱེད་རིམ་
kyilkhor	dkyil 'khor	དཀྱིལ་འཁོར་
lama	bla ma	བླ་མ་
lung	rlung	རླུང་
möpa	mos pa	མོས་པ་
ne ngen len	gnas ngan len	གནས་ངན་ལེན་
nepa	gnas pa	གནས་པ་

ngak	sngags	སྔགས་
ngöndro	sngon 'gro	སྔོན་འགྲོ་
nya ngen lay depa	mya ngan las 'das pa	མྱ་ངན་ལས་འདས་པ་
nyentö	nyan thos	ཉན་ཐོས་
nyönmong	nyon mongs	ཉོན་མོངས་
pakpay denpa shi	'phags pa'i bden pa bzhi	འཕགས་པའི་བདེན་པ་བཞི་
paröltu chinpa	pha rol tu phyin pa	ཕ་རོལ་ཏུ་ཕྱིན་པ་
pawo	dpa' bo	དཔའ་བོ་
pungpo nga	phung po lnga	ཕུང་པོ་ལྔ་
riktong yerme	rig stong dbyer med	རིག་སྟོང་དབྱེར་མེད་
rigpa	rig pa	རིག་པ་
rinchen	rin chen	རིན་ཆེན་
roma	ro ma	རོ་མ་
sampten	bsam gtan	བསམ་གཏན་
sang-gye	sangs rgyas	སངས་རྒྱས་
selwa	gsal ba	གསལ་བ་
sem	sems	སེམས་
shepa	shes pa	ཤེས་པ་
sherab	shes rab	ཤེས་རབ་
she shin	shes bzhin	ཤེས་བཞིན་

161

shi-ne	zhi gnas	ཞི་གནས་
shinjang	shin sbyangs	ཤིན་སྦྱངས་
shintu	shin tu	ཤིན་ཏུ་
shiwa	zhi ba	ཞི་བ་
soklung	srog rlung	སྲོག་རླུང་
sordu	sor sdud	སོར་སྡུད་
sosor tarpa	so sor thar pa	སོ་སོར་ཐར་པ་
tab lam	thabs lam	ཐབས་ལམ་
tekpa chenpo	theg pa chen po	ཐེག་པ་ཆེན་པོ་
tekpa chung	theg pa chung	ཐེག་པ་ཆུང་
tencho	bstan bcos	བསྟན་བཅོས་
tig-le	thig le	ཐིག་ལེ་
ting ngen dzin	ting nge 'dzin	ཏིང་ངེ་འཛིན་
tonglen	gtong len	གཏོང་ལེན་
tongpanyi	stong pa nyid	སྟོང་པ་ཉིད་
trömeh	spros med	སྤྲོས་མེད་
tsa	rtsa	རྩ་
uma	dbu ma	དབུ་མ་
yengwa	g.yeng ba	གཡེང་བ་
yeshe	ye shes	ཡེ་ཤེས་

Bibliography

Asanga. *Compendium of the Abhidharma*. Skt. *Abhidharmasamuccaya*; Tib. *mngon pa kun btus*.

———. *Levels of Śrāvakas*. Skt. *Śrāvakabhūmi*; Tib. *nyan sa*.

———. *Ornament of Clear Realization*. Skt. *Abhisamayālaṃkāra*; Tib. *mngon rtogs rgyan*.

Atiśa. *Lamp for the Path to Enlightenment*. Skt. *Bodhipathapradīpa*; Tib. *byang chub lam gyi sgron ma*.

———. *Quintessential Instructions on the Middle Way*. Skt. *Madhyamakopadeśa*; Tib. *dbu ma'i man ngag*.

Bodhibhadra. *The Prerequisites for Samadhi*. Skt. *Samādhisambhāra*; Tib. *ting nge 'dzin gyi tshogs*.

Chandrakīrti. *Entering into the Middle Way*. Skt. *Madhyamakāvatāra*; Tib. *dbu ma la 'jug pa*.

Jamgon Kongtrul. *Five Treasuries:*
1. *Treasury of Knowledge* (*shes bya mdzod*).
2. *Treasury of Kagyu Tantras* (*bka' brgyud sngags mdzod*).
3. *Treasury of Termas* (*rin chen gter mdzod*).
4. *Treasury of Instructions* (*gdams ngag mdzod*).
5. *Treasury of Vast Teachings* (*rgya chen bka' mdzod*).

Jñānagarbha. *Differentiation of the Two Truths*. *Satyadvayavibhaṅga*; Tib. *bden gnyis rnam par 'byed pa*.

Kamalaśila. *Stages of Meditation*. 3 vols. Skt. *Bhāvanākrama*; Tib. *sgom rim*.

Maitreya. *Differentiation of the Middle Way from the Extremes*. Skt. *Madhyāntavibhaṅga*; Tib. *dbu mtha' rnam 'byed*.

———. *Ornament of the Mahayana Sutras*. Skt. *Mahāyānasūtrālaṃkāra*; Tib. *theg pa chen po'i mdo sde'i rgyan*.

Bibliography

——. *Sublime Continuum of the Mahāyāna.* Skt. *Mahāyānottaratantra-śāstra;* Tib. *theg pa chen po rgyud bla ma'i bstan bcos.* English version: *The Changeless Nature,* trans. Katia and Ken Holmes (Kagyu Samye Ling, 1979).

Maitrīpa. *Commentary on the Ten Suchnesses.* Skt. *Tattvadaśaka;* Tib. *de kho na nyid bcu pa'i grel ba.*

Milarepa. *The Hundred Thousand Songs of Milarepa.* Tib. *mgur 'bum.* English version: 2 vols., trans. Garma C. C. Chang (Boston: Shambhala Publications, 1977, 1989).

Nāgārjuna. *Knowledge of the Middle Way.* Skt. *Mūlamadhyama-kakārikā;* Tib. *dbu ma rtsa ba'i shes rab.*

Rangjung Dorje (the third Karmapa). *The Mahāmudrā Prayer.* Tib. *phyag chen smon lam.*

Śāntarakṣita. *Adornment of the Middle Way.* Skt. *Madhyamakālaṃkāra;* Tib. *dbu ma'i rgyan.*

Śāntideva. *A Guide to the Bodhisattva's Way of Life.* Skt. *Bodhicaryāvatara;* Tib. *byang chub sems dpa'i spyod pa la 'jug pa.* English trans. Stephen Batchelor (Dharamsala: Library of Tibetan Works and Archives, 1982).

Sūtras

Cloud of Jewels. Skt. *Ratnameghasūtra;* Tib. *dkon mchog sprin gyi mdo.*

Definite Explanation of the View. Skt. *Saṃdhinirmocanasūtra;* Tib. *dgongs pa nges par 'grel pa' i mdo.*

Heart Sutra. Skt. *Mahāprajñāpāramitāhṛidayasūtra;* Tib. *bcom ldan 'das ma shes rab kyi pha rol tu phyin pa'i snying po'i mdo.*

About the Author

About five hundred years ago, the seventh Gyalwa Karmapa founded Thrangu monastery. He appointed as its abbot one of his most gifted disciples, the first Thrangu Rinpoche. More recently incarnations of Thrangu Rinpoche have spent much of their lives in retreat. The present ninth incarnation was recognized at the age of four in 1937 by the Gyalwa Karmapa and Palpung Situ Rinpoche, who prophesied the names of his parents and his place of birth.

In the time from the age of seven to sixteen Khenchen Thrangu Rinpoche learned to read and write, memorized pujas, and studied their practice. He then began his formal studies in Buddhist philosophy, psychology, logic, debate, and scriptures with Lama Khenpo Lodö Rabsel. At the age of twenty-three he received the Gelong ordination along with Garwang Rinpoche and Chögyam Trungpa Rinpoche from the Gyalwa Karmapa.

Following this, Thrangu Rinpoche engaged in a period of intense practice and retreat and received further instructions from his lama, Khenpo Gyangasha Wangpo. At the age of thirty-five he was given the degree of Geshe Ramjam with honors and was appointed Vice Chancellor of the Principal Seat of the Kagyü Vajra Upholder of the Three Disciplines by His Holiness Karmapa. He is full holder and teacher of all the Kagyü vajrayāna lineages and has a special, very direct transmission of the Shentong philosophical tradition. Being so gifted, he was chosen to educate the four great Kagyü regents.

About the Author

Thrangu Rinpoche has traveled extensively in Europe, the United States, Canada, and Asia. He has a three-year retreat center at Namo Buddha in Nepal, is in charge of long retreats at Samye Ling, Scotland, is abbot of Gampo Abbey in Canada, and offers yearly Namo Buddha Seminars for beginning and advanced students of Buddhism.

For more information on Thrangu Rinpoche's activities, contact the Namo Buddha Seminar, 1390 Kalmia Avenue, Boulder, CO 80304-1813.

Index

Index

Index

Index

sūtra tradition, 111–116
vajrayāna tradition, 116–119

vajrayāna approach, 80–81
vajrayāna tradition, 116–119
Vasubandhu, 8
vayū. *See* subtle airs
view, Buddhist, 67
vipaśyanā
    accomplishments of, 104–107
    of a bodhisattva, 75–80
    combined with śamatha, 12–13
    etymology of, 12
    four essences, 84–85
    four types of, 69–84
    of the mantrayāna, 80–84
    nonconceptual, 119–120

methods of, 93–104
prerequisites of, 65–69
six investigations, 86–92
of the śrāvaka, and pratyeka-
    buddha, 70–75
three categories of, 84–93
three doorways, 85–86
of a Tirthika, 69–70, 71
union with śamatha, 111–119
in the vajrayāna, 118–119
visualization stage, 133

wheel of existence, 114
wisdom, 148 n.12

yidam, 132–133